JN290889

MUTTONI Café

by Muto Masahiko

ムットーニ・カフェ

武 藤 政 彦

工作舎

Aの書斎よりムットーニへ

とうとう書斎が届きました。
もう目がかすんでしまった老博士が
それでも本にすがって生きていますね。
でも12時の鐘が鳴ったとき、
ほんの一瞬、幼かった頃の博士が
幻として現れます。
少年はつめたく、未来の自分をみつめます。
この人は本をよみすぎて年老いた、と。
たぶん、これはだれもが通る道でしょう。
おいぼれなければ、人生のドラマなんて生まれないのですから。
ムットーニはいつも、ふりかえりながら未来を見せてくれる。
まるで、過去のように手の届かない未来を。

荒俣宏

From A's Library to Muttoni

At last, the Library arrived.

Though his eyes have grown dim, the old professor still clings to his books.

But when the clock strikes 12, a vision of himself as a young boy appears for a moment.

The boy looks coldly upon his future self.

That man has grown old by reading too many books, he thinks.

Maybe that is the road we all must wander.

Because unless we grow old, there would be no drama to life.

Muttoni always shows us the future by looking back.

A future that is out of reach, just like the past.

Aramata Hiroshi

MUTTONI Café
menu

message　Aの書斎よりムットーニへ From A's Library to Muttoni
　　　　　荒俣宏 Aramata Hiroshi ……… 002

café outside

星の記憶 on the planet

　　摩天楼2000 Skyscrapers 2000 …………… 008
　　『月世界探検記』(海野十三) Gessekai-Tanken-Ki …………… 014
　　楽士 Musicista …………… 020
　　クリスタル・ランデブー Crystal Rendez-Vous …………… 023
　　メランコリー・ヴィーナス Melancholy Venus …………… 026
　　トップ・オブ・キャバレー The Top Of The Cabaret …………… 029
　　やがて鐘が鳴る When The Bell Tolls …………… 033
　　クリスタル・キャバレー Crystal Cabaret …………… 036
　　二つの夜 Two Nights …………… 041

cover: Winter Voyager (1999)

café anotherside
自鳴琴の祭 in the carnival of musical boxes
踊る犬 Dancing Dog ················046
カエル使い Frog Master ················047
猫と菓子 Dish Dinner ················048
ランデブー Rendez-Vous ················049
アンドロイドの夢 The Android's Dream ················050
アンドロイドの調整 Android Inspection ················052
衛星のヴィーナス Station Venus ················054
ミイラ男の目覚め Deep Waking ················055

café inside
夜半物語 around midnight
書斎 Library ················058
『猫町』（萩原朔太郎）Neko-Machi ················065
『山月記』（中島敦）Sangetsu-Ki ················071
グロリア・マリアが来たりて Here Comes Gloria Maria ················077
ドラキュラの晩餐 Last Supper ················086
透明人間の帰還 Return Home ················091
バニーズ・メモリー Bunny's Memory ················098

afterword　あとがき———武藤政彦 Muttoni ················108

005
MUTTONI Café
menu

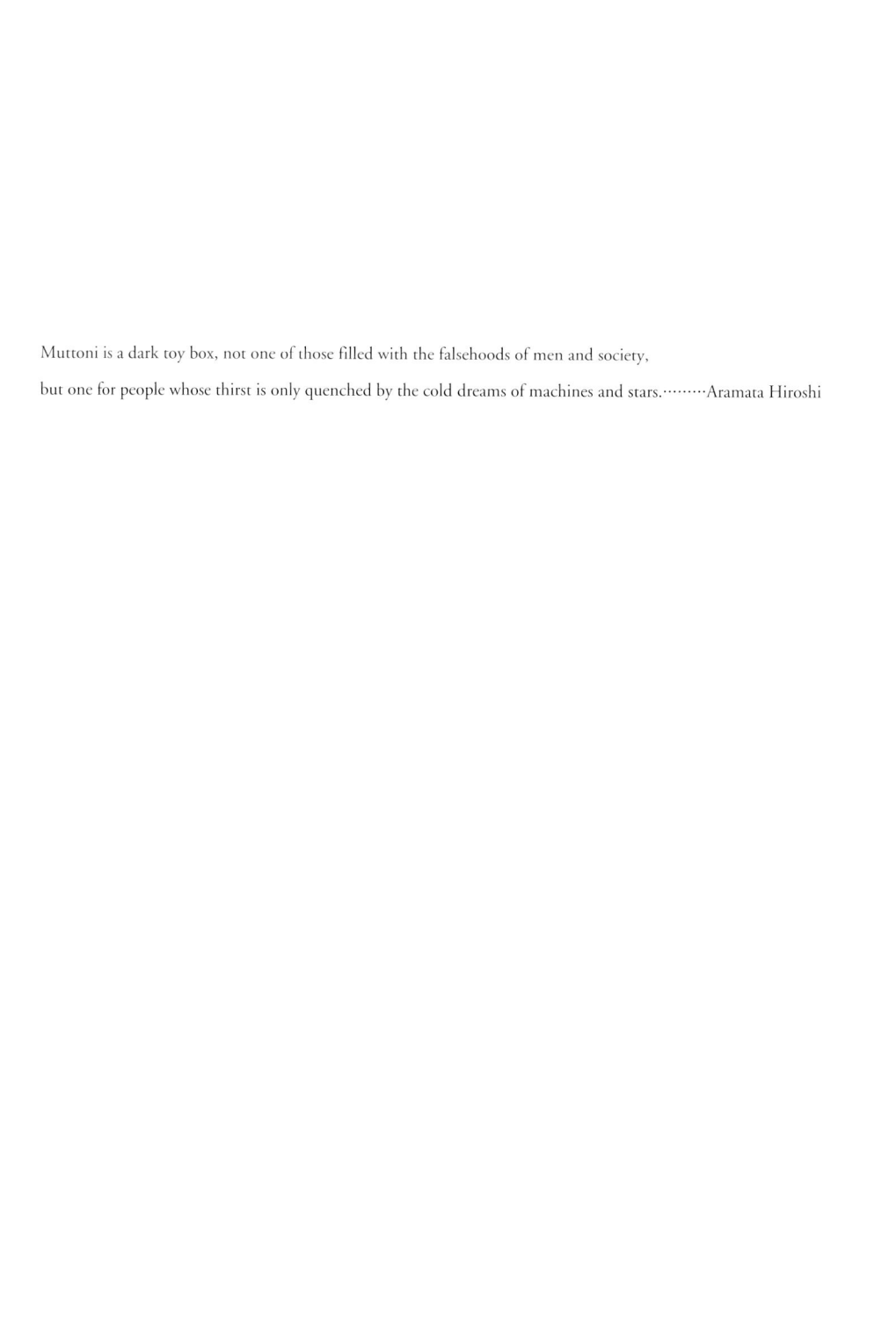

Muttoni is a dark toy box, not one of those filled with the falsehoods of men and society,

but one for people whose thirst is only quenched by the cold dreams of machines and stars.·········Aramata Hiroshi

café outside

星の記憶

on the planet

Skyscrapers 2000
摩天楼2000

1999
sound: Richie Cole "If Ever I Would Leave You"

林立する摩天楼を臨む小さな公園。
ベンチで寄り添う一組のカップル。
昇りはじめた太陽は世界を光で満たし、
ベンチはゆっくりとまわり出す。

A small park in front of a skyskraper jungle.
A couple snuggle up on a bench.
As the rising sun fills the world with light,
the bench slowly starts to turn.

008
café outside
Skyscrapers 2000

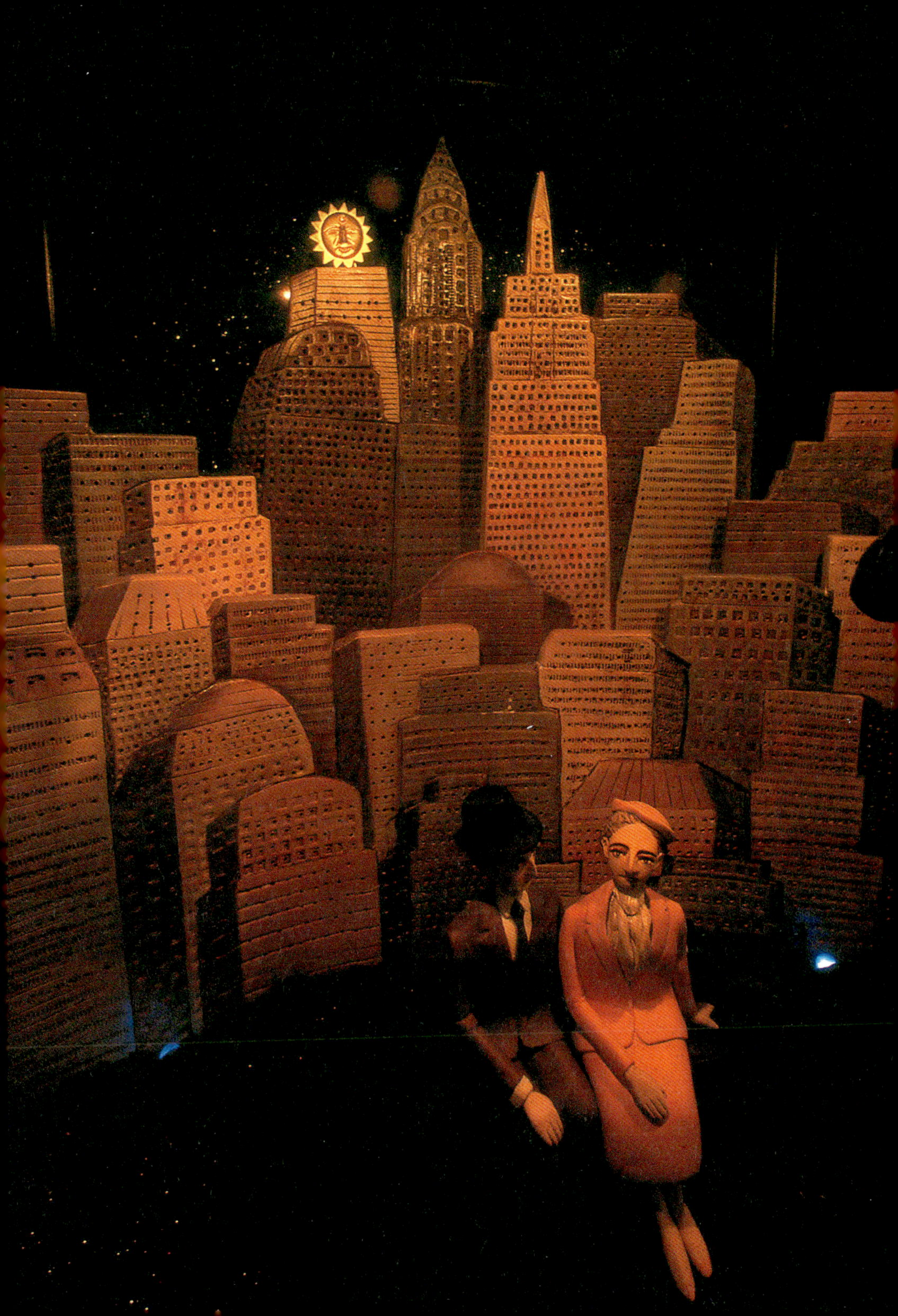

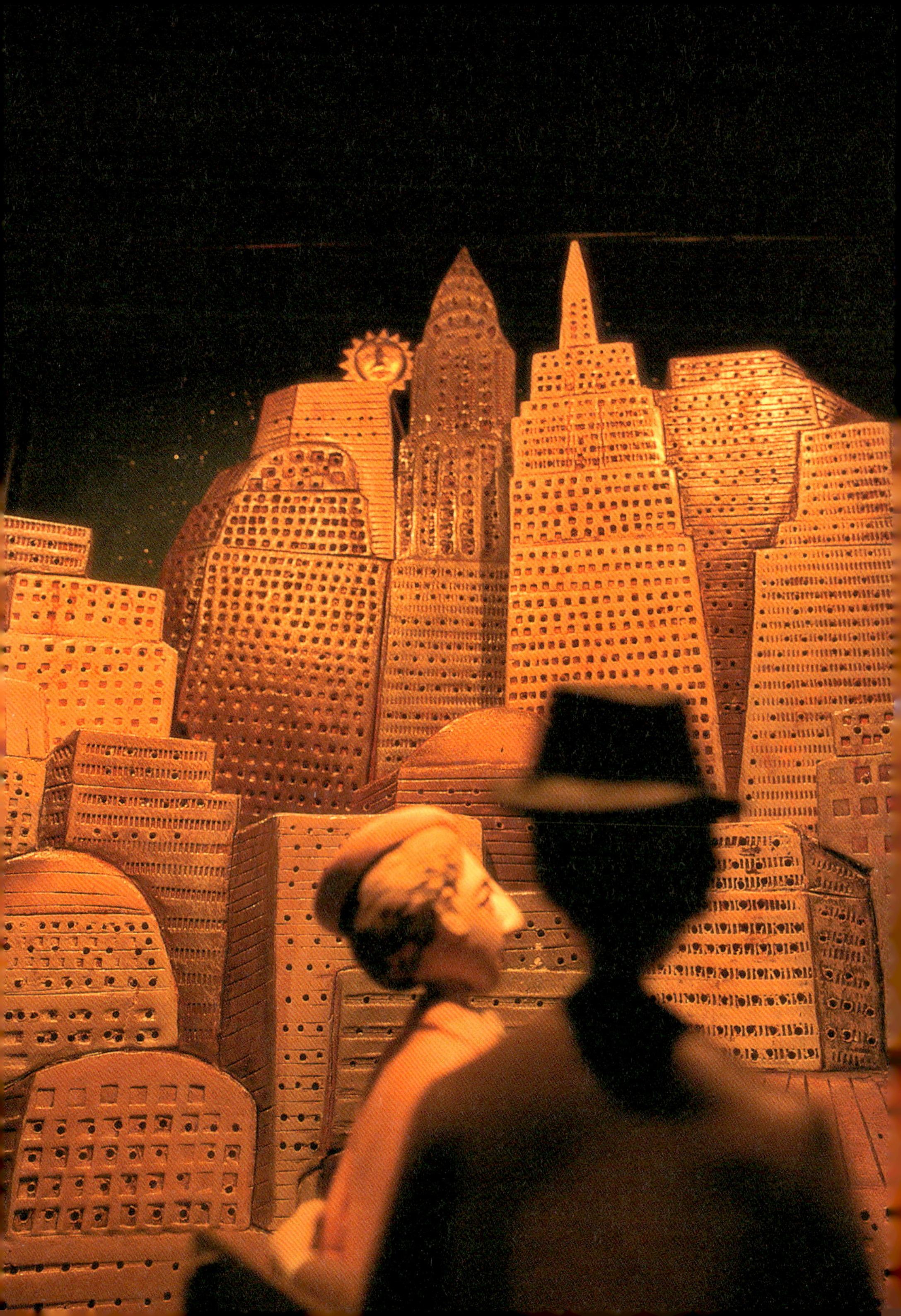

都会の空はやがて夕日に染まり、
太陽はビルの谷間へと沈んでゆく。

The city sky takes on the tones of dusk,
as the sun sets in the valley between the buildings.

ビルの窓に灯がともり、
外灯の光を受けながら
なおもベンチは回りつづける……。

The lights go on in the windows,
and under the streetlights
the bench keeps on turning...

café outside
Skyscrapers 2000

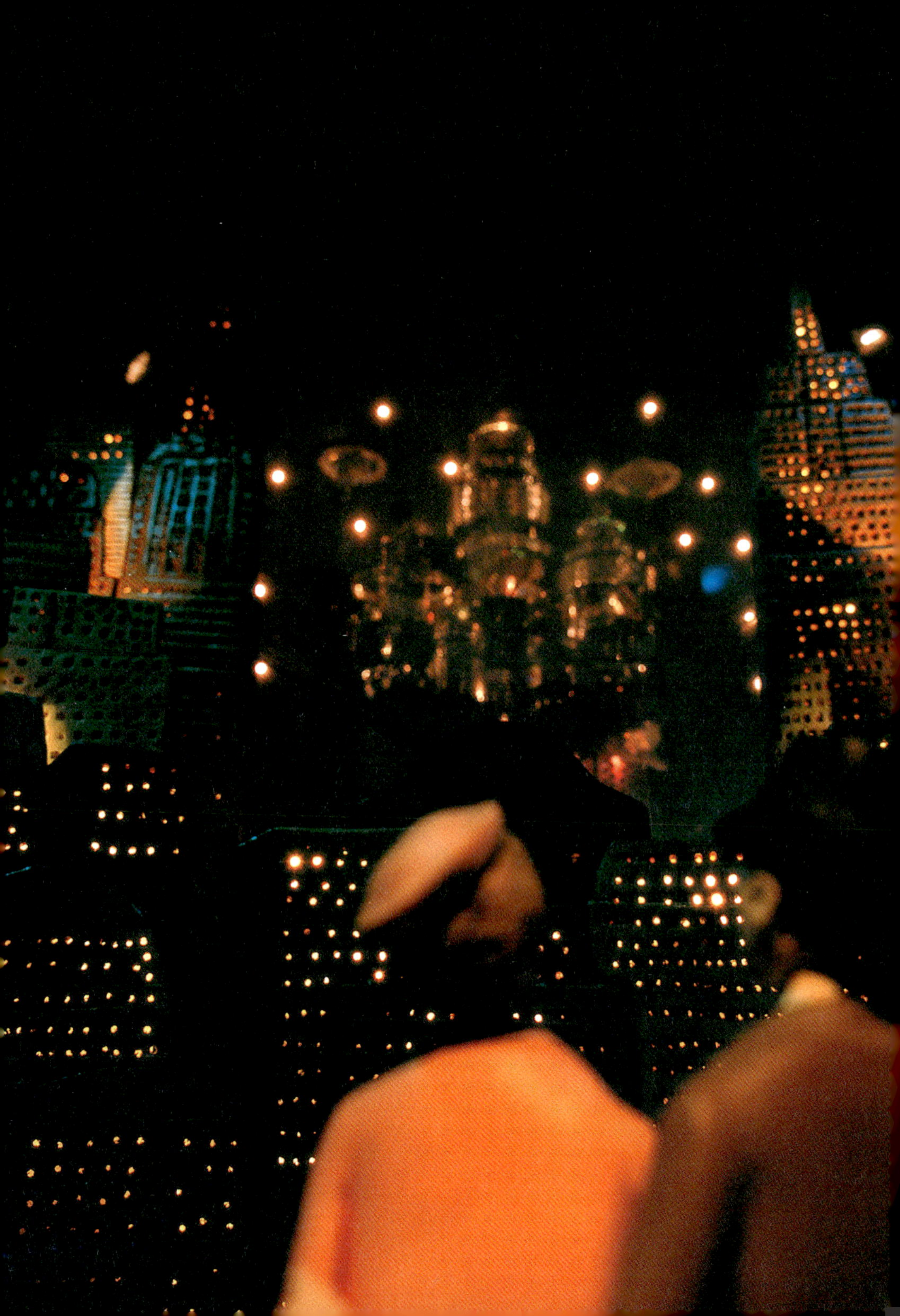

しかし、こんな光景も、カップルも、もしかするとそのすべては、
すっかりその姿を変えてしまった未来都市が見ている、
想い出の一場面であるのかもしれない。

But maybe this scene, and the couple and everything else,
is just a memory in the mind of a future city,
that now has changed beyond recognition.

013
café outside

Skyscrapers 2000

Gessekai-Tanken-Ki [Lunar Explorers]
『月世界探検記』(海野十三)

1995
original sound: RA（guitar & synthesizer）
owned by: Setagaya Literary Museum

014
café outside
Gessekai-Tanken-Ki

二人は今、月世界に立った。
聳える宇宙都市。輝くドーム。
その遥か彼方を
惑星たちがゆっくりと回っている。

A couple is standing on the moon.
A soaring space city. Sparkling domes.
And far in the distance,
the planets slowly revolve.

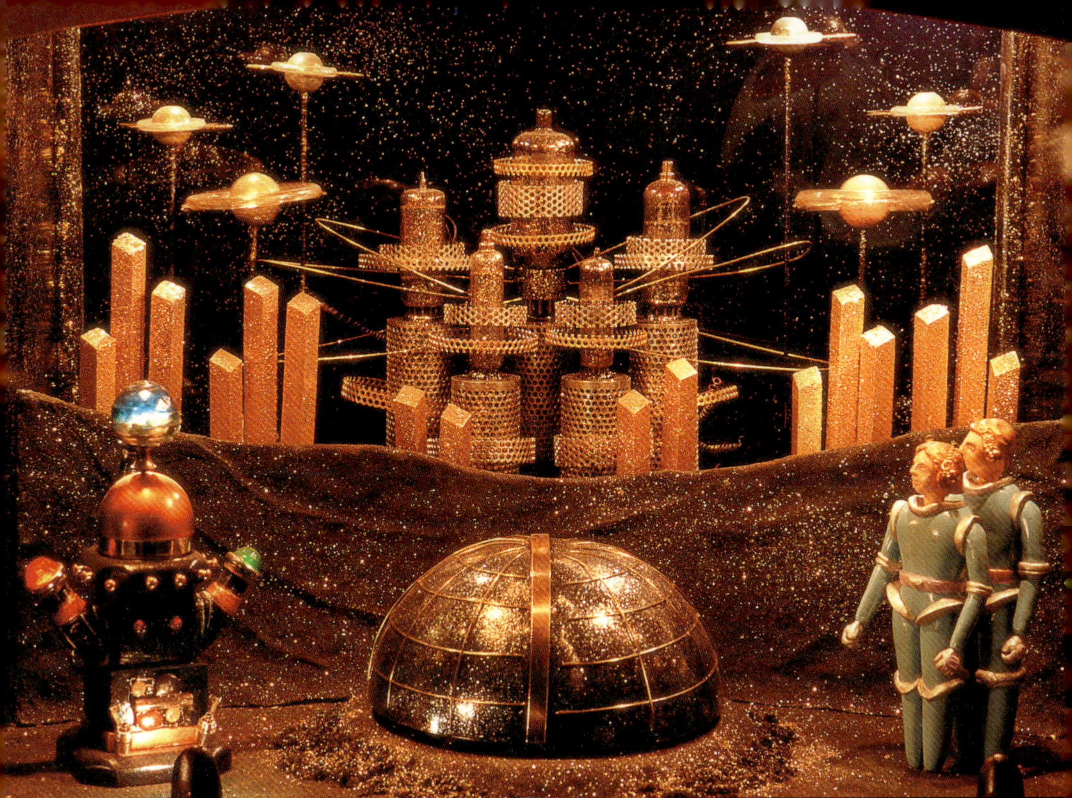
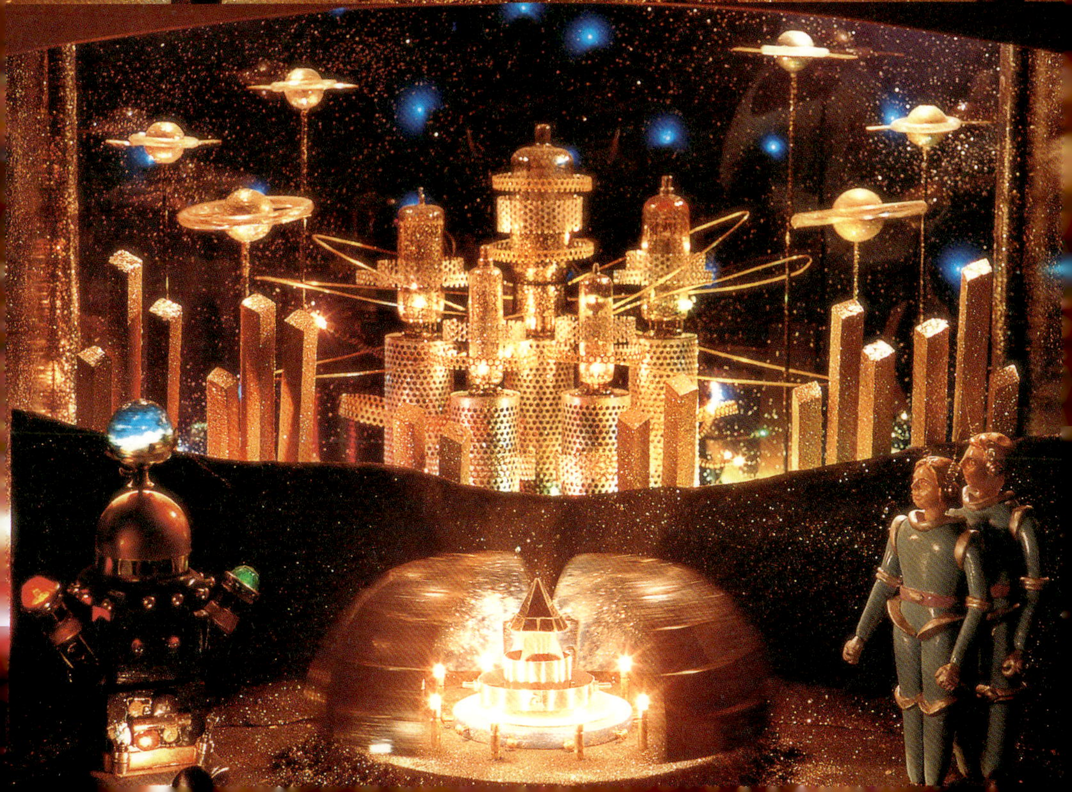

銀色のドームが二つに割れ、
宇宙に向けてロケットが翼を開く。

The silver dome splits in half,
and a rocket spreads its wings
towards the stars.

016
café outside
Gessekai-Tanken-Ki

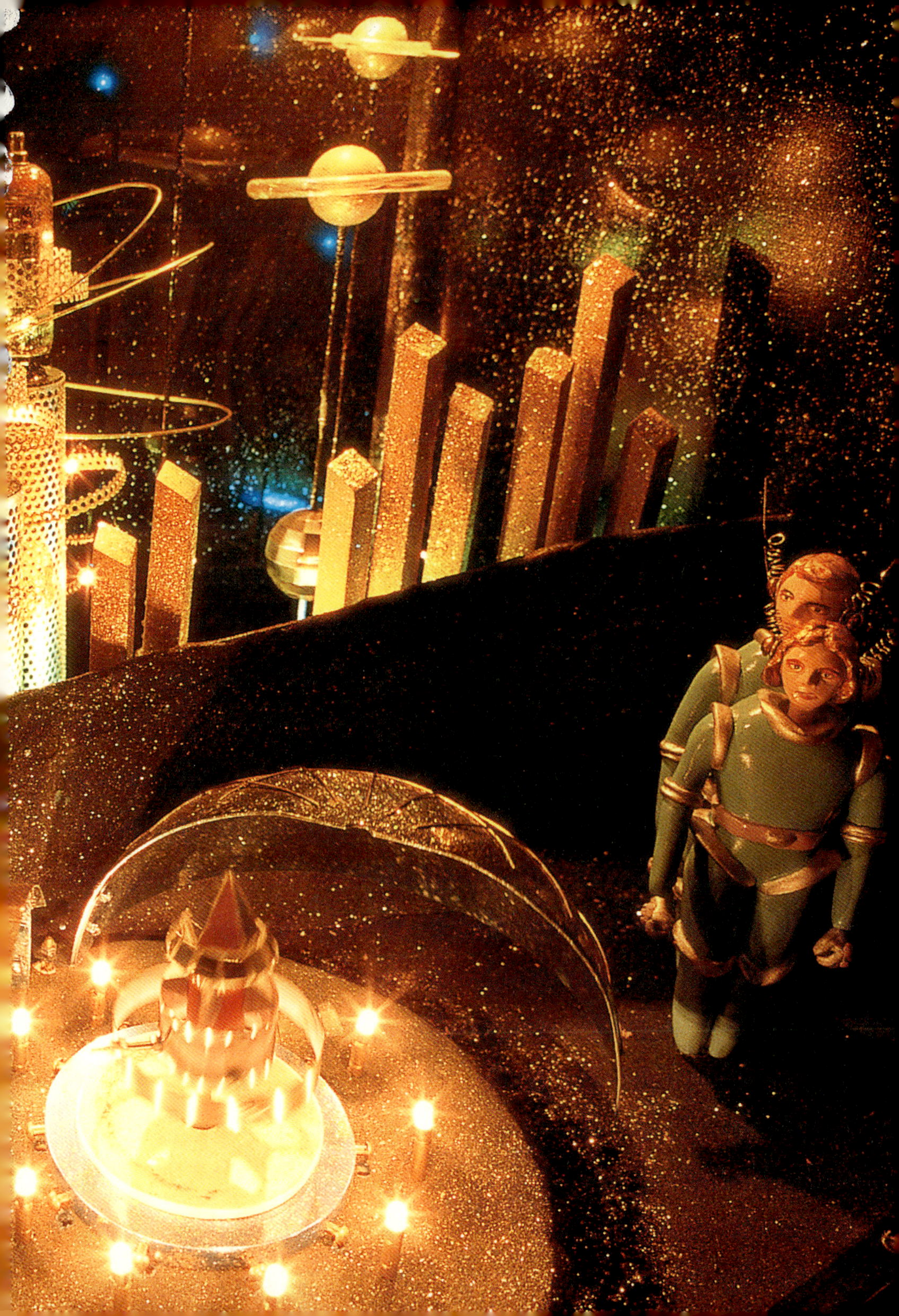

上昇したロケットは光を放ち、
世界にメッセージを送る。
今、宇宙を見つめる二人の目に映るのは、
トルコ石めく地球の姿……。

The rocket takes off, radiating light,
sending messages to the world.
Now, as the couple look out into space,
their eyes reflect the turquoise gleam of Earth...

018
café outside
Gessekai-Tanken-Ki

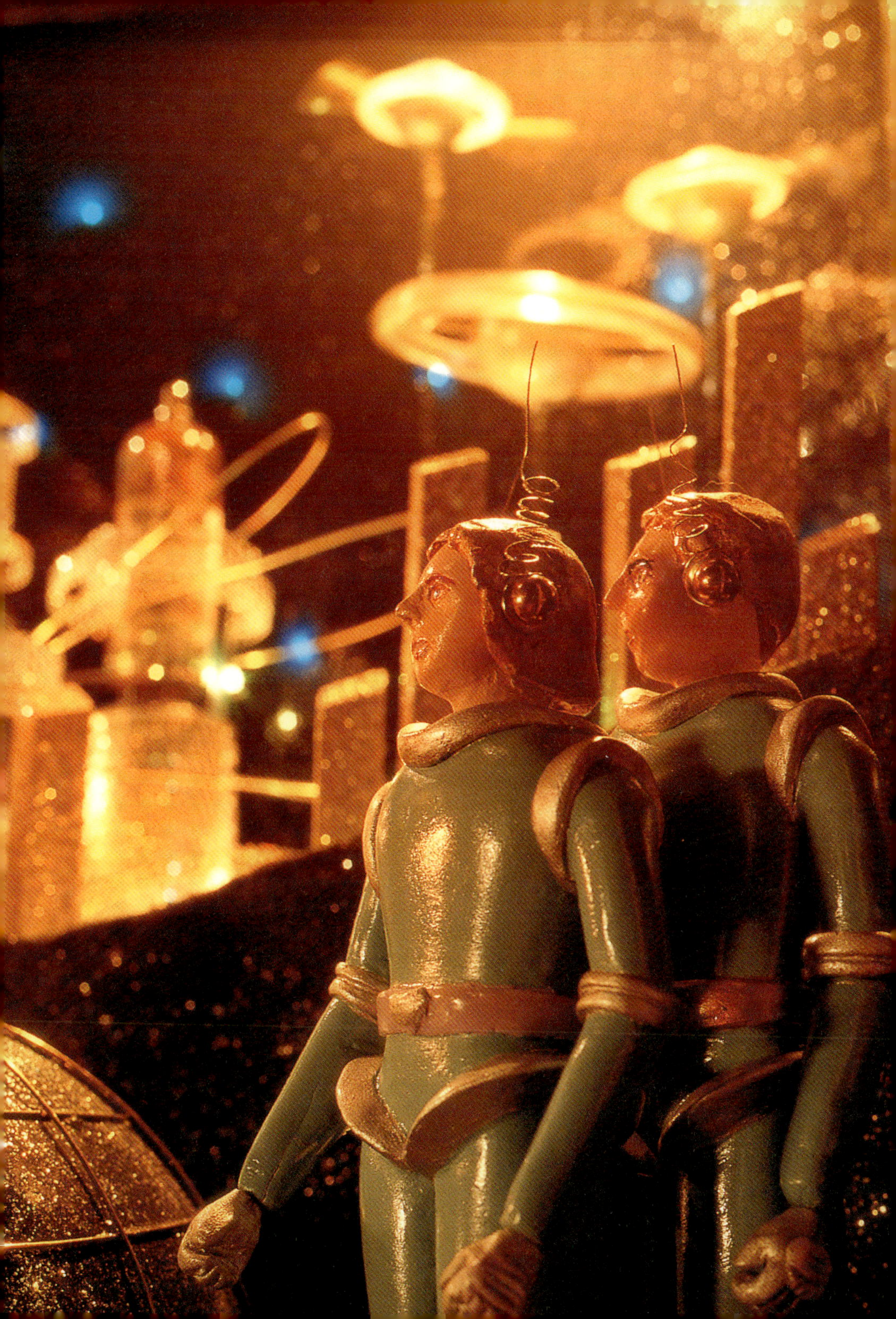

Musicista
楽士

1997
sound: Arthur H "Je Rêve De Toi"
owned by: Matsuda Yukimasa

国を超え、様々な街を訪ね歩く一人の楽士。
今宵はここがねぐらと定め、
傍らにランプをともす。

The musician wanders from city to city,
from country to country.
Tonight I will lay my hat here, he decides,
and a street lamp lights up beside him.

café outside
Musicista

そしてこの日最後の歌を、
自分のために歌いはじめる。

And then he starts to sing the final song for the night,
only for himself.

022
café outside
Musicista

夜空に星が瞬く頃、
思いもかけぬ一人の観客が、
孤独な楽士に
ひとときの幸福をもたらした。

By the time the stars start to twinkle in the sky,
an unexpected visitor arrives,
bringing a moment of bliss to the lonely musician.

Crystal Rendez-Vous
クリスタル・ランデブー

1999
sound: Dinah Shore "My Melancholy Baby"

023
café outside
Crystal Rendez-Vous

想い出の結晶に囲まれ、
彼女は夜の底で光を放つ。

Surrounded by crystals of memories,
she illuminates the depth of the night.

café outside
Crystal Rendez-Vous

光はいくつもの時を超え、
忘れられた惑星のカップルに注がれる。

Sent out by lovers on forgotten planets,
the light has transcended eons.

……それは光の幻。そして彼女の夢。

...An illusion of light. And also her dream.

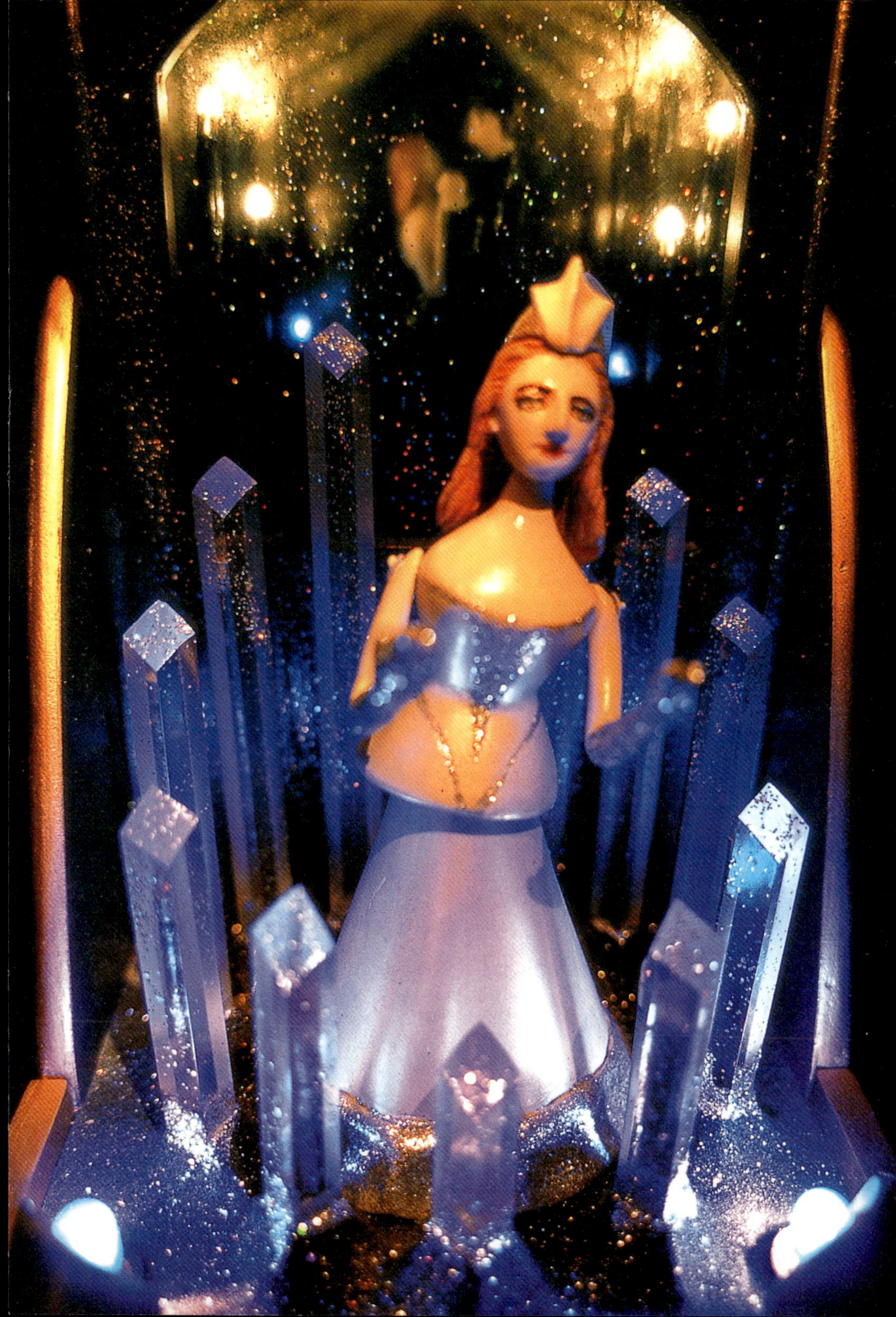

Melancholy Venus
メランコリー・ヴィーナス

1997
sound: Ernestine Anderson "My Melancholy Baby"
owned by: Yamaguchi Jun

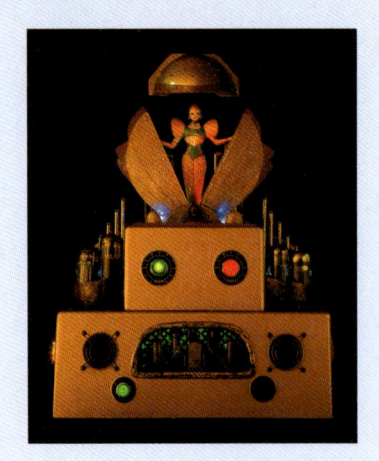

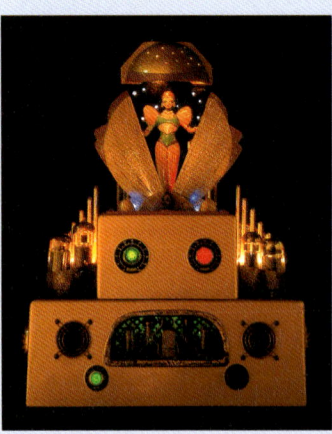

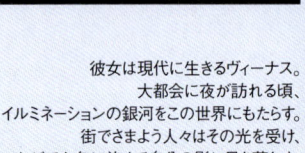

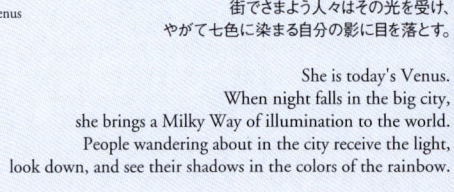

026
café outside
Melancholy Venus

彼女は現代に生きるヴィーナス。
大都会に夜が訪れる頃、
イルミネーションの銀河をこの世界にもたらす。
街でさまよう人々はその光を受け、
やがて七色に染まる自分の影に目を落とす。

She is today's Venus.
When night falls in the big city,
she brings a Milky Way of illumination to the world.
People wandering about in the city receive the light,
look down, and see their shadows in the colors of the rainbow.

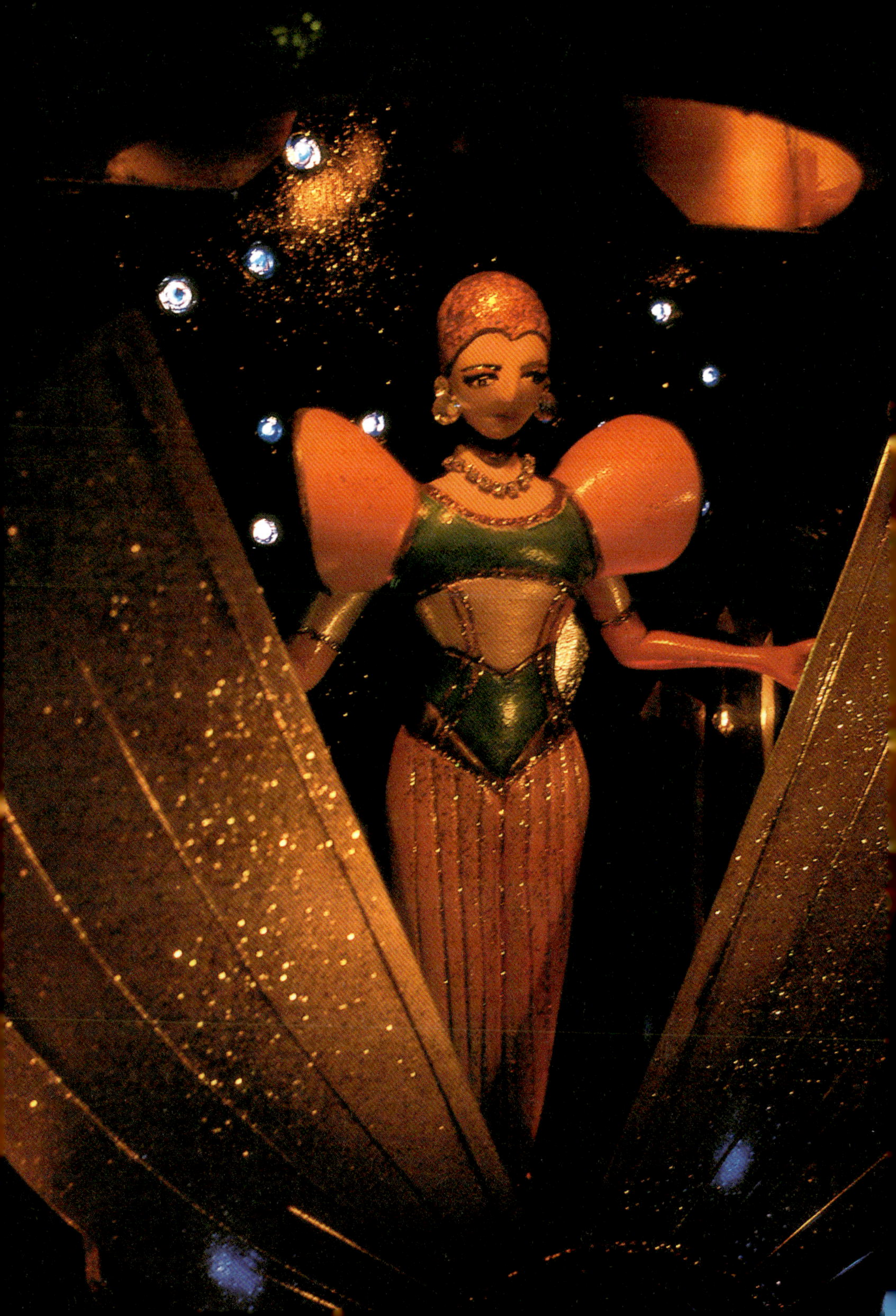

その姿を隠す間際に、
彼女はもう一度光を放ち、
今日の終わりを美しく飾る。

As she hides herself again,
she sends out a final ray of light,
bringing the day to an exquisite close.

028
café outside
Melancholy Venus

The Top Of The Cabaret
トップ・オブ・キャバレー

1997
sound: Harry James Orchestra (vo: Kitty Kallen)
"Like The Moon Above You"

酒もホロ酔い、今日は自然に体が乗ってくる。
こんなときは、JAZZ！　楽しむのなら、
やっぱりBIG BAND！
そして今宵の歌姫は……。

The moonshine tastes bittersweet.
Tonight, the body wants to hang loose.
At times like this, the music is jazz!
Nothing can compare to a big band!
And tonight's nightingale is...

029
café outside
The Top Of The Cabaret

café outside
The Top Of The Cabaret

歌姫が振り向き、バンドの面々にスタートの合図を送る。
やがてトランペッターにスポットライトが当たり、
いよいよトップ・オブ・キャバレーの開幕。

The singer turns around, and the band members exchange signals.
The spotlight falls on the trumpeter,
and at last the cabaret begins.

トランペッターがソロをとる中、
ステージには、ダンサーたちが登場。
ショータイムが盛り上がる。

As the trumpeter plays his solo,
dancers appear on the stage,
livening up the show.

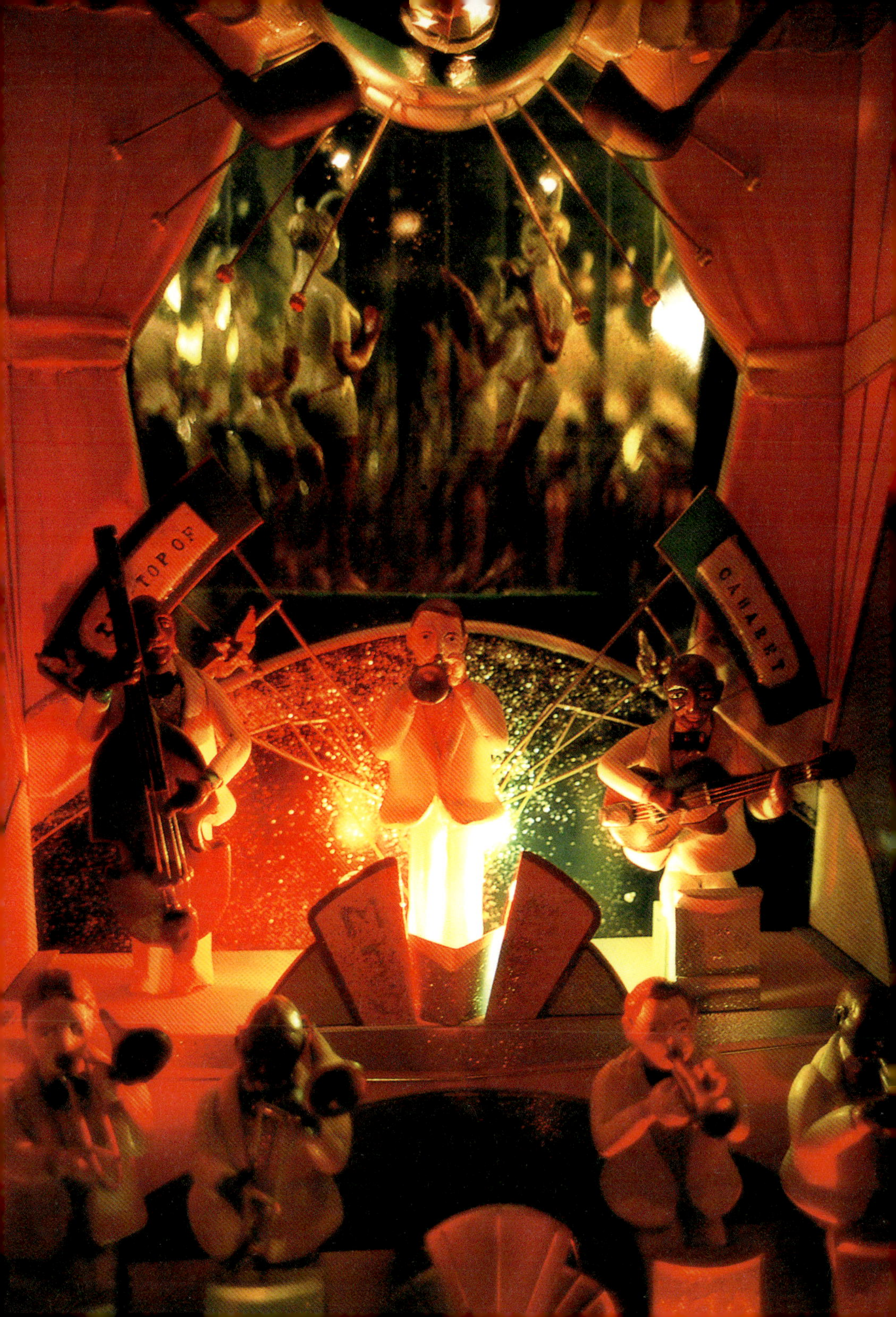

個性豊かなバンドの面々。
トランペッター、サックス吹きにベーシスト。

The guys in the band are all real cool cats.
The trumpeter, the sax player, the bassist.

032
café outside
The Top Of The Cabaret

ジャズのサウンドの中に、
多彩な個性が溶けてゆく。
そしてエンディングは、フルパワーで。

In the sound of the jazz,
their multicolored styles blend together.
And the ending is at full blast.

When The Bell Tolls
やがて鐘が鳴る

1994
sound: Elizabeth Cardoso "Camari"
owned by: Aramata Hiroshi

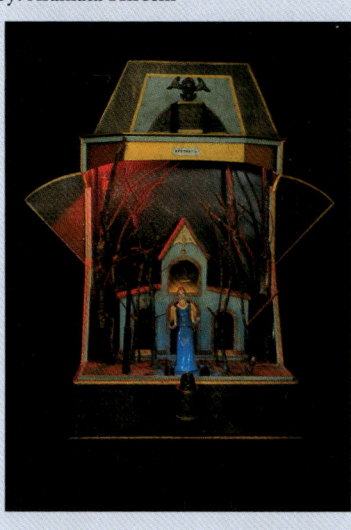

きらびやかなステージとスポットライトを逃れ、
彼女は今、一人の旅人として
教会の前にたたずむ……。

Away from the gaudy stage and the spotlights,
she is now a lone traveler
lingering in front of a church...

033
café outside
When The Bell Tolls

やがてあたりは夕陽に染まる。
教会の鐘が鳴り響く頃、彼女は気づく。
今、自分が美しく静かな眼差しの中で
歌っていることを……。

As the sunset colors the surroundings,
and the church bell starts to toll,
she notices how she is singing
in the beautiful, quiet gaze of another...

café outside
When The Bell Tolls

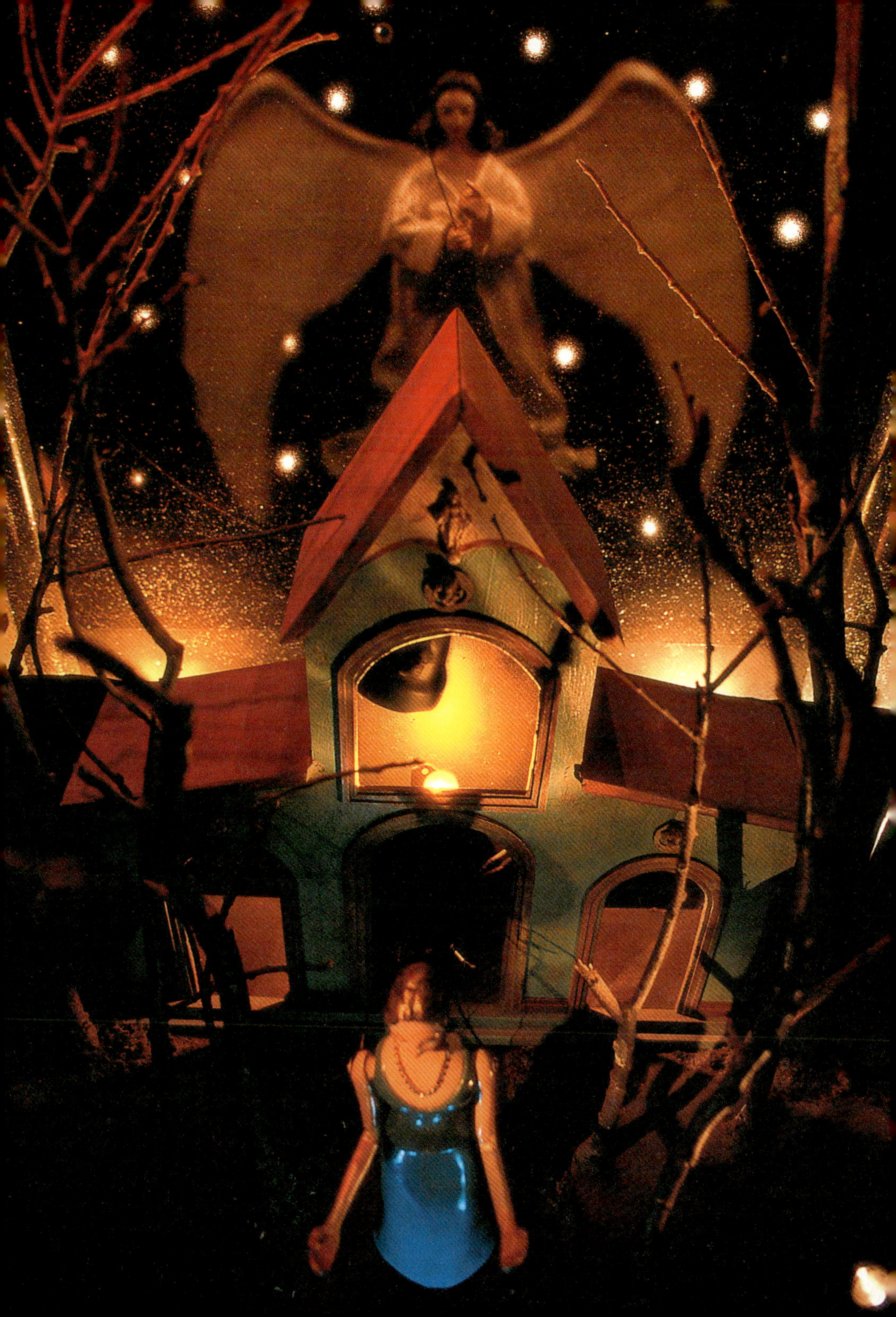

Crystal Cabaret
クリスタル・キャバレー

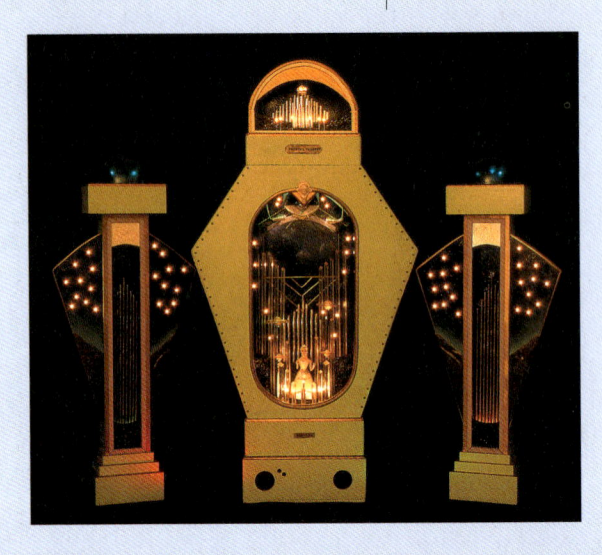

1995-6
sound: Dinah Shore "My Melancholy Baby"

名もない小さな惑星に、彼女のために作られた
一夜かぎりの特別ステージ、クリスタル・キャバレー。
「今宵こそあなたが歌姫。
あなたの息吹きは光となって世界を満たす。
今宵こそあなたが歌姫……」

On a small planet without so much as a name,
Crystal Cabaret is a special stage built only for her,
only for tonight.
"Tonight you are our nightingale.
Your breath is the light that fills the world.
Tonight you are our nightingale..."

036
café outside
Crystal Cabaret

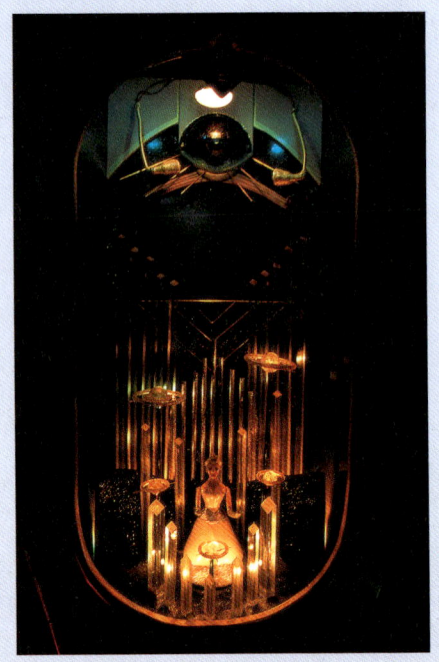

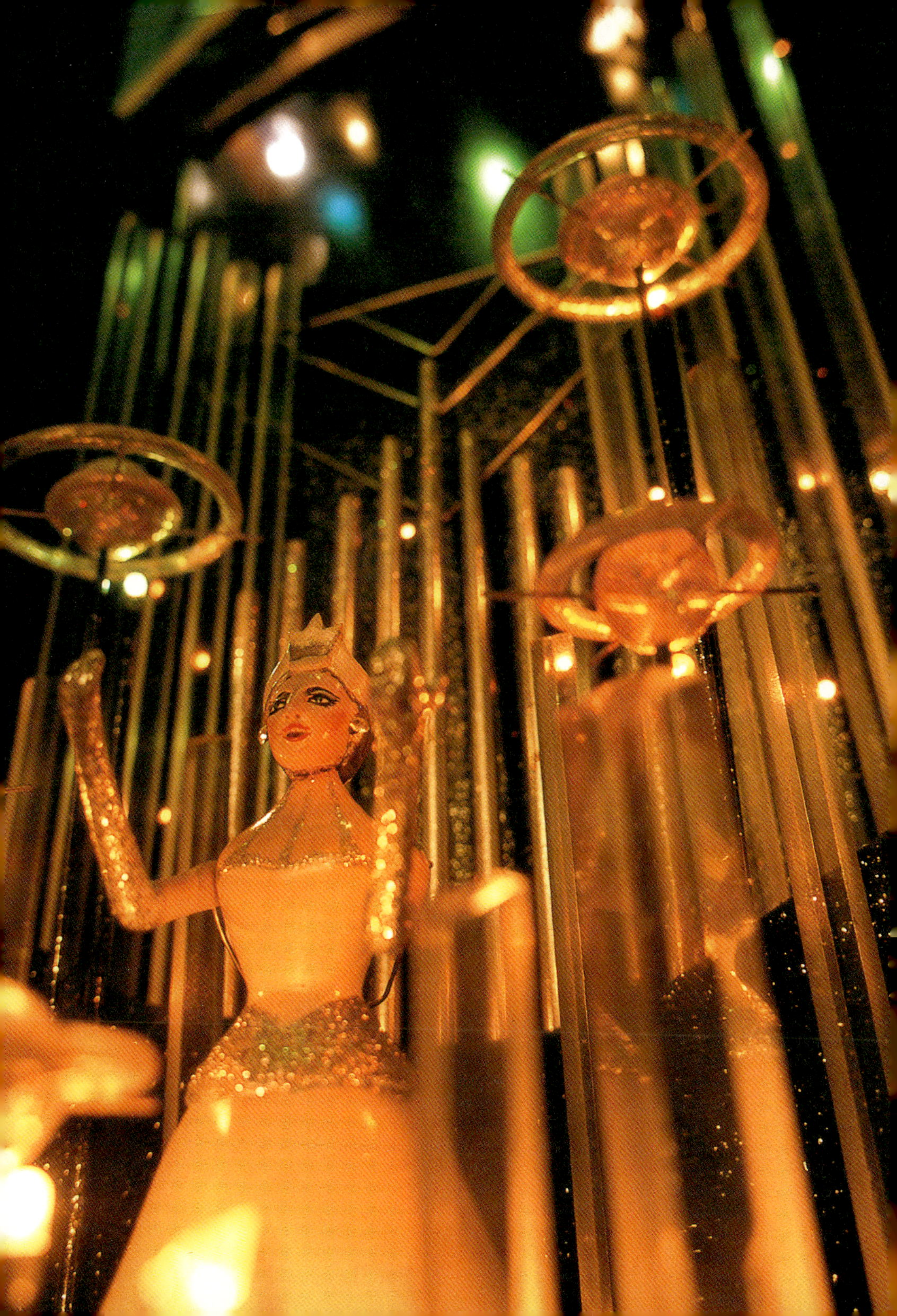

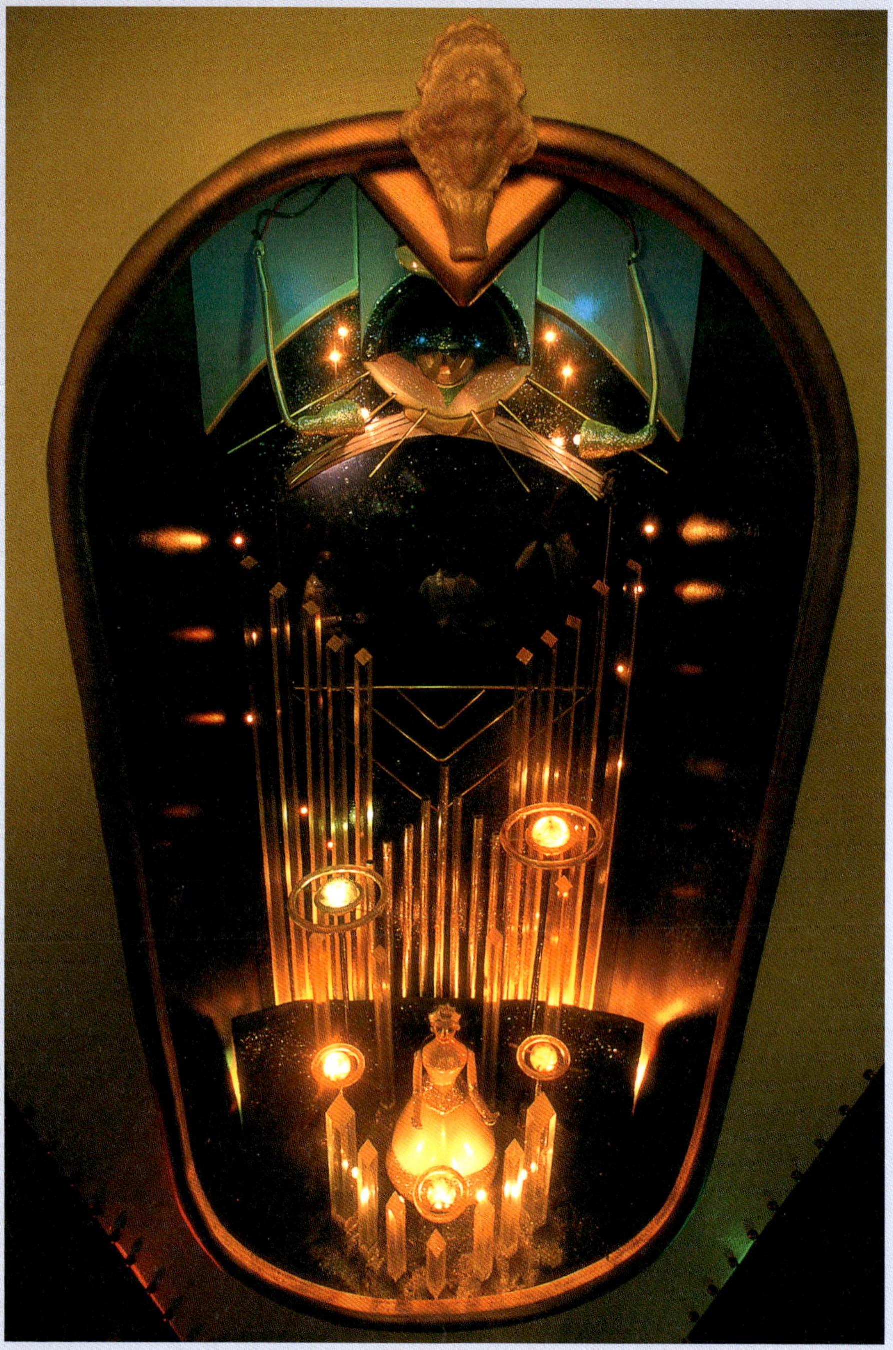

宇宙の片隅に煌めく夜が訪れて、
ピアノ・トリオが彼女をもり立てる。

In the glittering night in a corner of the universe,
a piano trio backs her up.

039
café outside
Crystal Cabaret

「今宵こそあなたが歌姫。
時と光が、あなたのまわりで交差する。
今宵こそあなたが歌姫。
時と光が、あなたを中心にめぐりはじめる」

"Tonight you are our nightingale.
Time and light intersect beside you.
Tonight you are our nightingale.
Time and light circulate around you."

Two Nights
二つの夜

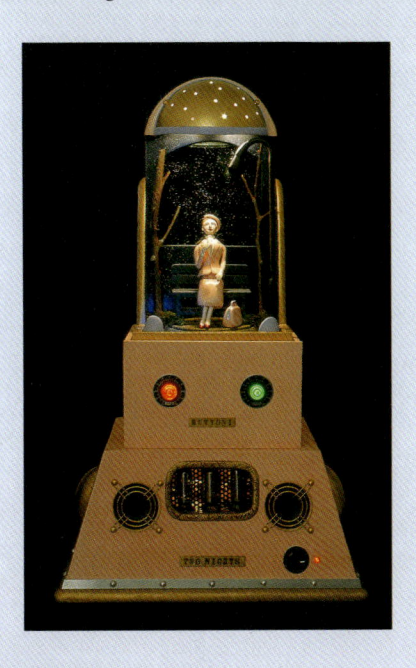

1999
sound: Patti Page "It's A Sin To Tell A Lie"

旅行鞄を足元に、
ベンチで想いにふける一人の女性。
外灯に火がともる頃、
彼女が夢見るもう一つの夜……。

A woman lost in reveries on a bench
with her suitcase by her feet.
As the streetlights come on,
she dreams about another night...

041
café outside
Two Nights

彼女は思う。
「あれは想い出、それとも予感……」

"Was that a memory," she wonders,
"or perhaps a premonition...?"

042
café outside
Two Nights

その瞬間、遠く離れた惑星で、
一組のカップルが彼女のことを
思い描いているとも知らずに……。

What she doesn't know is that at the very same moment,
on a planet far, far away,
another couple is fantasizing about her...

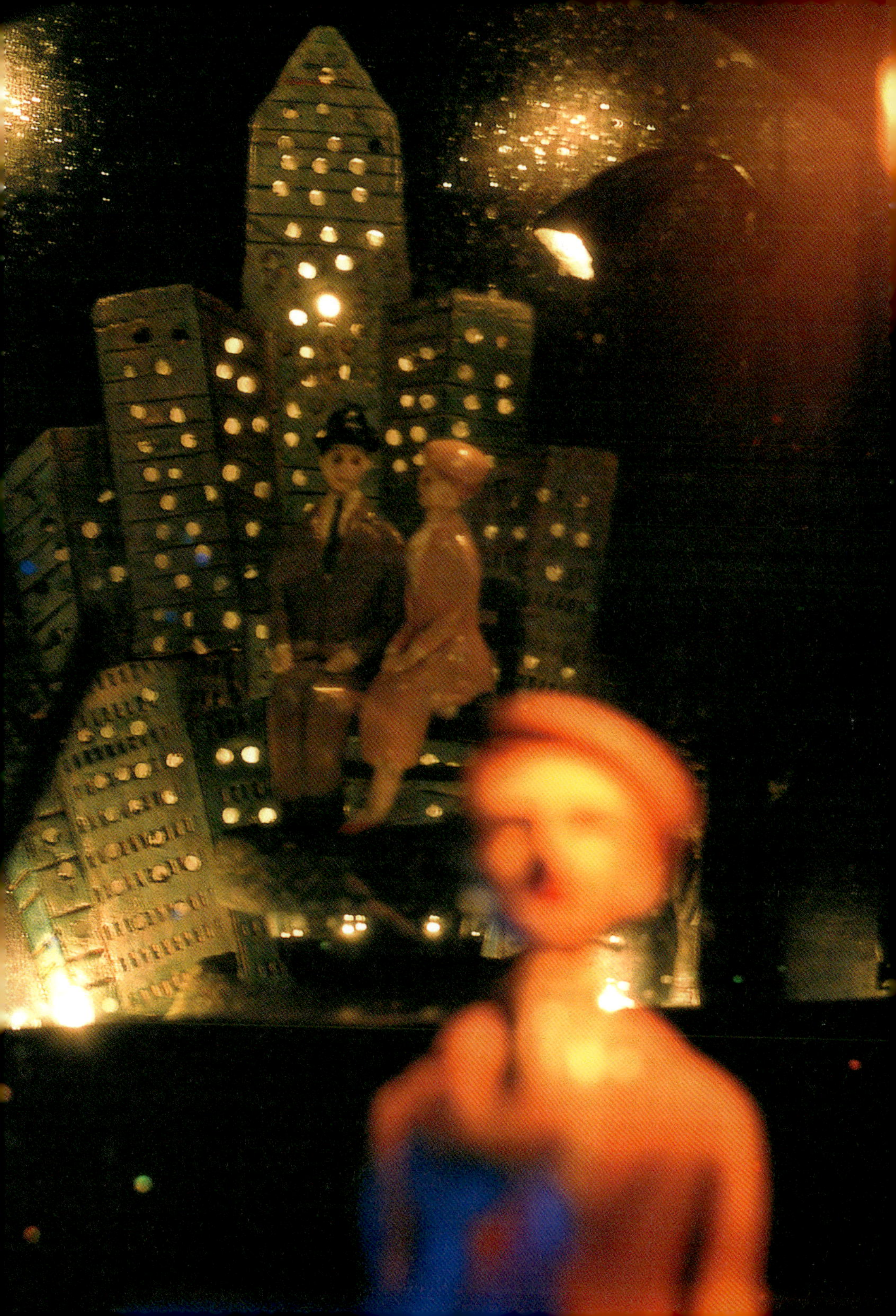

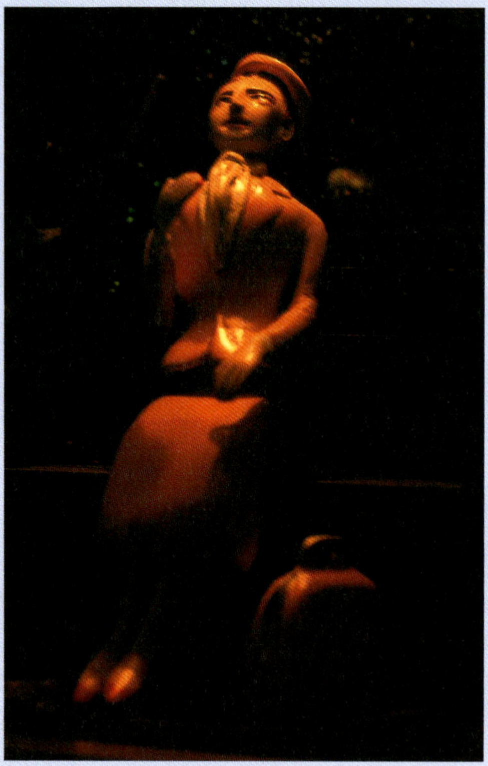

café anotherside

自鳴琴の祭

in the carnival of musical boxes

Dancing Dog
踊る犬

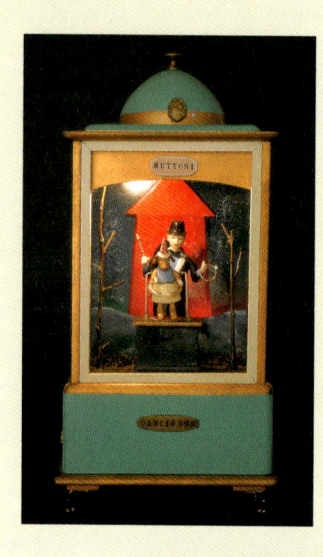

1996
wind-up spring
owned by: Yamaguchi Jun

男は職も家族もすべてを失い、ローマの街中をぶらついていた。
真夜中、とある路地に差し掛かったとき、
男はそこで一匹の犬と運命的な出会いを果たす。
翌朝、ヨレヨレのベビー服と小さなフラフープが入った鞄を片手に、
一匹の犬を連れて、男は旅に出た。

This man has lost his job and his family,
and wanders about the streets of Rome.
Late one night, as he turns into an alley,
he encounters a dog that will change his life.
The next morning he sets out on a journey with the dog,
and a suitcase filled with threadbare baby clothes
and a small hula-hoop.

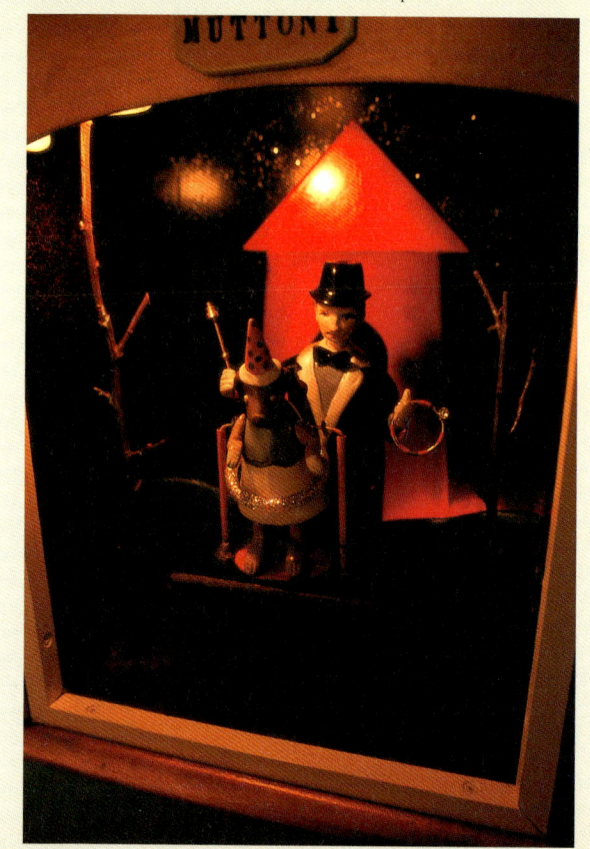

café anotherside
Dancing Dog

Frog Master
カエル使い

| 1996
wind-up spring
owned by: Yamaguchi Jun

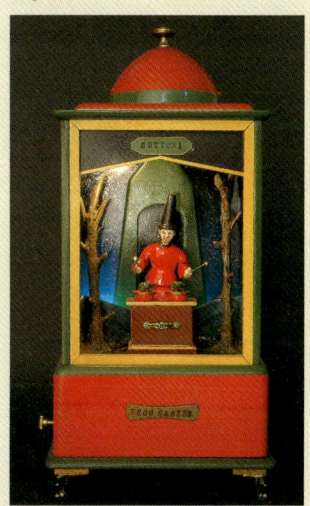

林の奥から雨垂れのような不思議な音が響く。
「ピタッ　ピタッ　ピタッ……」
どうやらまた、あの男がカエルを踊らせているらしい。

Deep in the woods echoes the mysterious sound of dripping water.
"Drip... drip... drip..."
It seems like *that man* is making the frogs dance again.

047
café anotherside
Frog Master

Dish Dinner
猫と菓子

1996
wind-up spring
owned by: Yamaguchi Jun

048
café anotherside
Dish Dinner

猫はケーキを食べようと、
皿の上に飛び乗った。
堂々めぐりの皿回し。
いつになっても食べられない。

Hungry for cake,
the cat jumped onto a plate.
But the plates keep turning
so that he never gets to eat it.

Rendez-Vous
ランデブー

1998
musical box
owned by: Yamaguchi Jun

宇宙飛行士は遊泳中に妄想を抱いた。
「宇宙には中心とリズムがあり、
我々はそれに操られて、
同じ所をグルグル回る……」
アンドロイドはサックスを演奏しながら思った。
「ワタシハイマ、ウチュウノチュウシンニイル」

The astronaut on his spacewalk has a fantasy:
"There is a center of the universe, and it's got rhythm,
and it keeps us revolving 'round the same place."
And the android, playing his sax, thinks:
"I am now at the center of the universe."

049
café anotherside
Rendez-Vous

The Android's Dream
アンドロイドの夢

1995
musical box
owned by: Yamaguchi Jun

050
café anotherside
The Android's Dream

彼は日夜、宇宙の中心で舵を取る。
この世界のバランスを保つため……。

Day and night he holds the wheel at the center of the universe,
to keep the world in balance...

だが人々は彼のことを、宇宙の果ての
世を捨てた孤独な舵取りと思うかもしれない。

But maybe people think of him as just a lonely steersman
who has renounced the world at the edge of the universe.

café anotherside
The Android's Dream

Android Inspection
アンドロイドの調整

1999
musical box

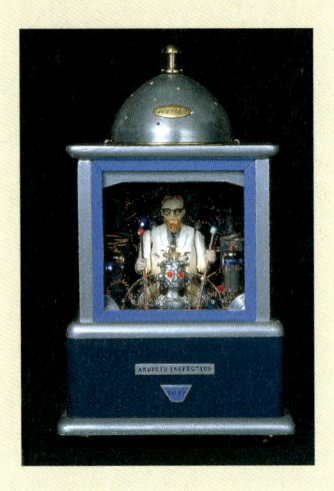

ほの暗くあやしげな実験室で、
博士は今日もアンドロイドを調整する。

In his shady laboratory,
the professor is adjusting androids as usual.

052
café anotherside
Android Inspection

もっとも、アンドロイドの目に何が映っているのか、
博士はとんと知らないけれど……。

But what is the android seeing?
As to that, the professor hasn't got a clue...

053
café anotherside
Android Inspection

Station Venus
衛星のヴィーナス

1999
musical box

054
café anotherside
Station Venus

多くの人間が危険を冒し、宇宙へと旅立ってゆく。
彼等は知っているのだろうか。
行き着く先はみな、私のもとだということを……。

Many people brave great dangers to travel into space.
But I wonder if they know that wherever they go,
I have already been there...

Deep Waking
ミイラ男の目覚め

1999
original sound: Muttoni (sampling & voice)

深い眠りから目覚めたミイラ男。
彼は世界を見渡すために、
その両目を掌に移植した。

The mummy awoke from his deep sleep,
and transplanted his eyes to his hands
to look out over the world.

055
café anotherside
Deep Waking

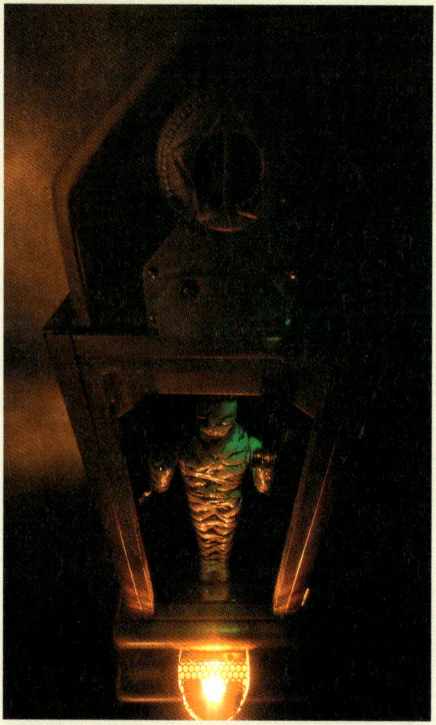

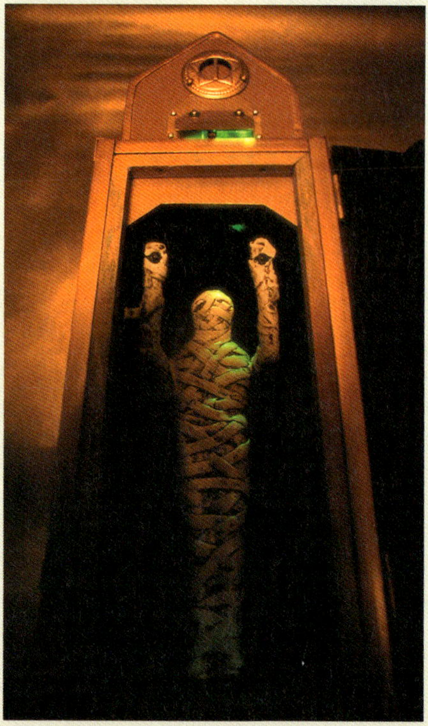

café inside

夜半物語

around midnight

Library
書斎

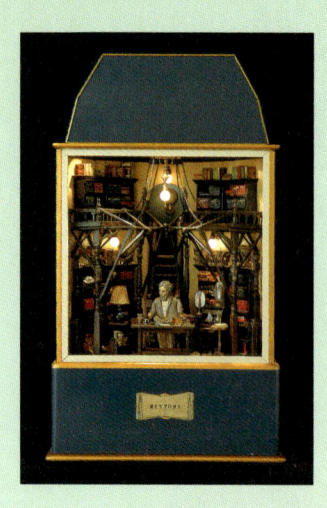

1997
original sound: Muttoni (keyboard, synthesizer & voice)
owned by: Aramata Hiroshi

累々たる書物に囲まれた部屋に、時計の音が響く。
皮装の書物を机の上に開け、読みふける一人の老人。

A clock tick-tocks in a book-lined room.
An old man sits absorbed in a leather-bound tome.

いつしか老人は聞きとれぬほど低い声で、
独り言をつぶやきはじめる。
やがて時計の鐘が真夜中を告げ、
老人は束の間の幻想を垣間見る。

Suddenly he starts mumbling
in an almost inaudible voice.
As the clock strikes midnight
He glimpses a mirage among the bundles.

059
café inside
Library

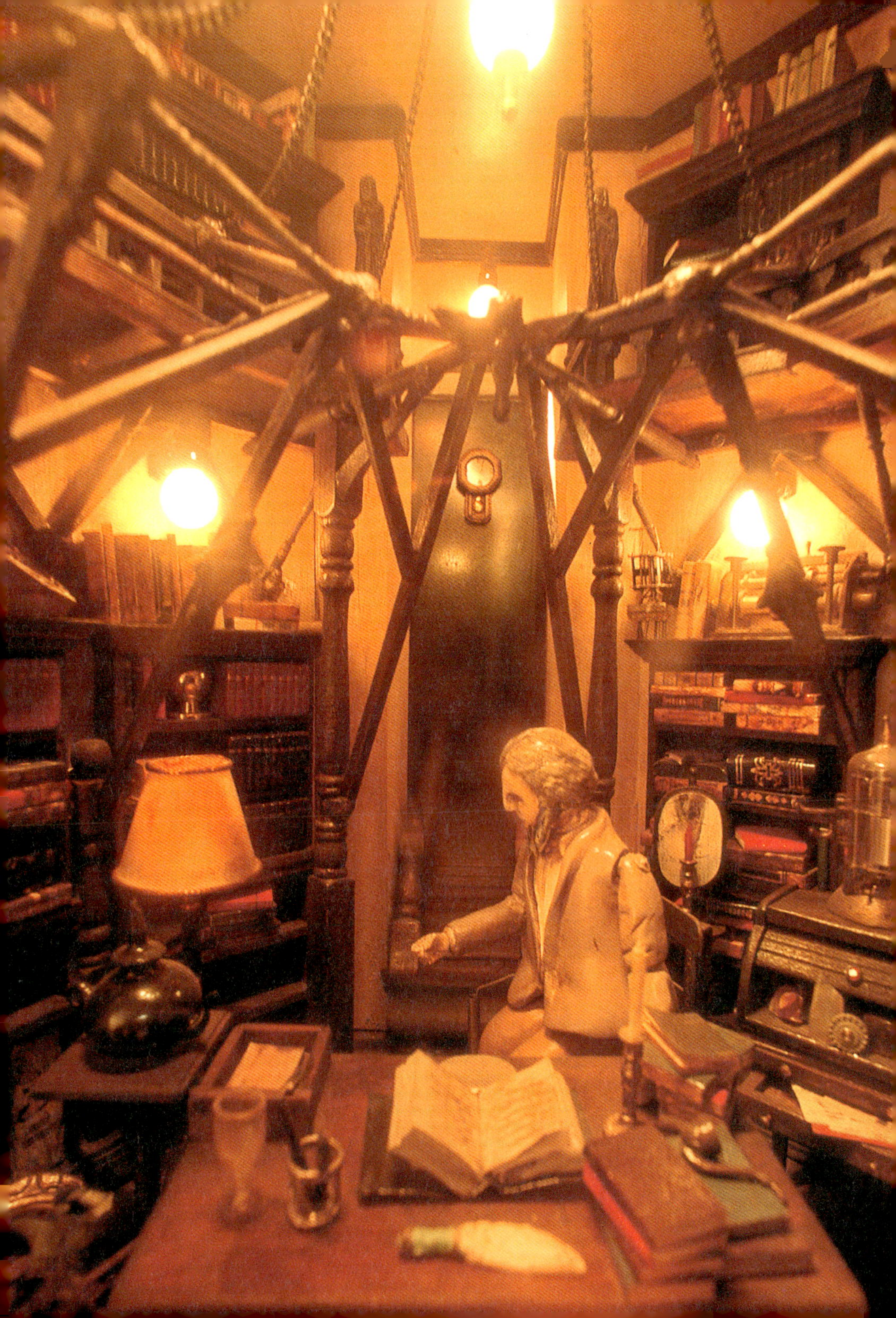

軋みを上げながらゆっくりと階段を降りると、
その奥に一人の少年の姿が浮かび上がる。

As he descends the creaking stair,
he sees a boy facing away.

振り向く少年。
それは、はじめて書物と出会った頃の自分自身。

The boy turns around.
It is himself,
at the age when he first discovered writing.

061
café inside
Library

しかし、老人に注がれる少年の眼差しは冷たい。
記号の累積と化した書物から、
何の感動も得られなくなってしまった、
今の自分を悲しむかのように……。

But the boy's look on the old man is cold,
as if he felt sorry for his later self,
for whom writing has become just a bunch of symbols
that no longer move him...

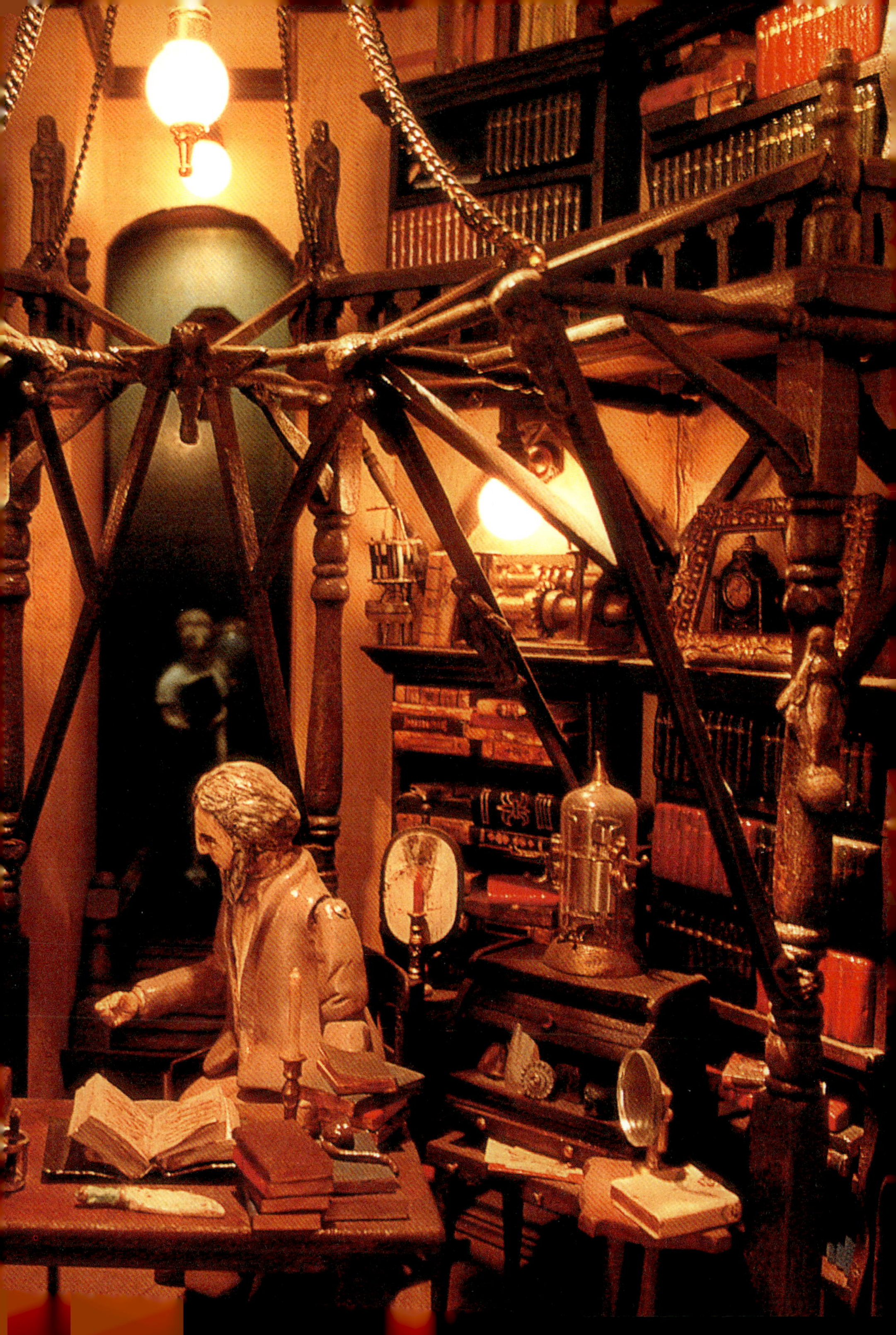

累々たる書物の屍。机に向かう一人の老人。
時を刻む時計の音だけが、書斎に響く。

In a room lined with dead books, an old man sits in front of his desk.
The only sound in the library is the tick-tock of the clock, counting out time.

Neko-Machi [Cat City]
『猫町』(萩原朔太郎)

1995
original sound & narration: Muttoni
(keyboard, clarinet & synthesizer)
owned by: Setagaya Literary Museum

065
café inside
Neko-Machi

男は山の麓まで来たとき、
幻灯のような風景に出会った。
そこには貧しい農家の代わりに
美しい街があった。
そして男は、
その幻灯の中へと入っていった。

As the man arrived at the foot of the mountain
he found a scene like in a magic lantern.
Instead of a poor farm, there was a beautiful city.
So the man entered the magic lantern.

街は何処も繊細で、
非常に人為的に構成されていた。
ちょっとしたバランスを失っても
粉々に崩れてしまう。
男はそのことに気づいたとき、
異常な緊張の中で焦燥した。
「いまだ!」
恐怖に胸を動悸しながら、思わず
男が叫んだとき……。

The city was very delicate
and looked extremely artificial.
As if everything might crumble
if you lost your balance even slightly.
The unnatural tension made him uneasy.
"Now!" he couldn't help shouting,
his heart throbbing with fright.

街のあちこちからあらわれる猫。
そこに人の姿はなく、猫ばかりで
溢れかえっていた。

From every corner of the city, cats appeared.
Not a single human being could be seen,
only an abundance of cats.

068
café inside
Neko-Machi

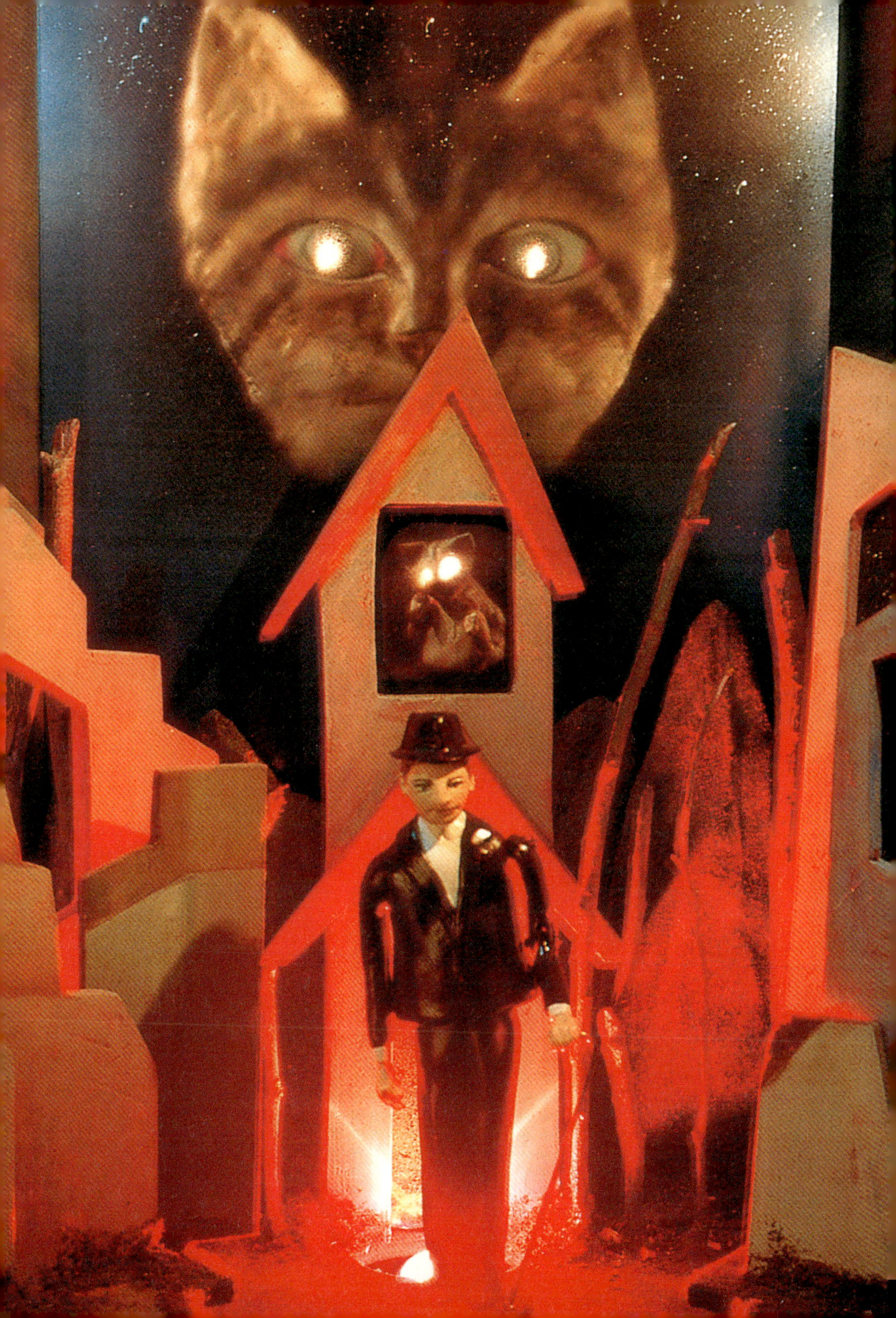

男の幻想はここで終わる。
人はこの男の話を、愚にもつかない妄想の幻影だという。
だが男は今も堅く心に信じている。
宇宙のどこかに、猫の精霊ばかりが住んでいる街が、
かならず実在しているということを。

Here ended the man's vision.
People say that his story is just a ridiculous fantasy.
But deep in his heart, he still firmly believes
that somewhere in the universe there is a city
where only the ghosts of cats reside.

café inside
Neko-Machi

Sangetsu-Ki [On A Moonlit Mountain]
『山月記』(中島敦)

1995
original sound: Muttoni (guitar, flute & sound effects)
narration: Kasahara Takuro
owned by: Setagaya Literary Museum

071
café inside
Sangetsu-Ki

袁傪(えんさん)は使命を帯び道を急いだ。
まだ夜も明けぬうちに、
人食い虎が出るという山中へと
足を踏み入れた。

Ensan hurried along on his appointed task.
Before the break of dawn he entered the mountains
where a man-eating tiger was said to appear.

月明かりを頼りに、
一行は林間の草地にさしかかった。

With only the moonlight to guide them,
the group entered the forest path.

072
café inside
Sangetsu-Ki

そのとき、一匹の猛虎が草むらから躍り出て、
あわや袁傪に飛び掛かると見えたが、
たちまち身をひるがえし、もとの草むらに隠れた。
草むらからは、「あぶないところだった」と、
しきりに繰り返す人間の声が聞こえた。

073
café inside
Sangetsu-Ki

At that moment, a wild tiger jumped out of the thicket
and was just about to pounce on Ensan,
when all of a sudden he turned around
and hid back in the thicket whence he had come.
From the thicket a human voice could be heard
repeating "That was close, that was close."

「その声は我が友、李徴ではないか」
「いかにも、自分は隴西の李徴である」
袁傪は恐怖を忘れ、馬から降りて草むらに近づいた。

"That voice, if it isn't my old friend Lichou."
"Indeed I am Lichou from Rousai."
Ensan forgot his fear, descended from his horse and approached the thicket.

李徴は今にいたるまでの
いきさつを語りはじめた。
やがてあたりの暗さが薄らいだ頃、
李徴は林間の奥深くへとその姿を消した。

Lichou started to tell the events
that had befallen him up to the present.
Then, when the darkness grew lighter,
he disappeared deep into the forest.

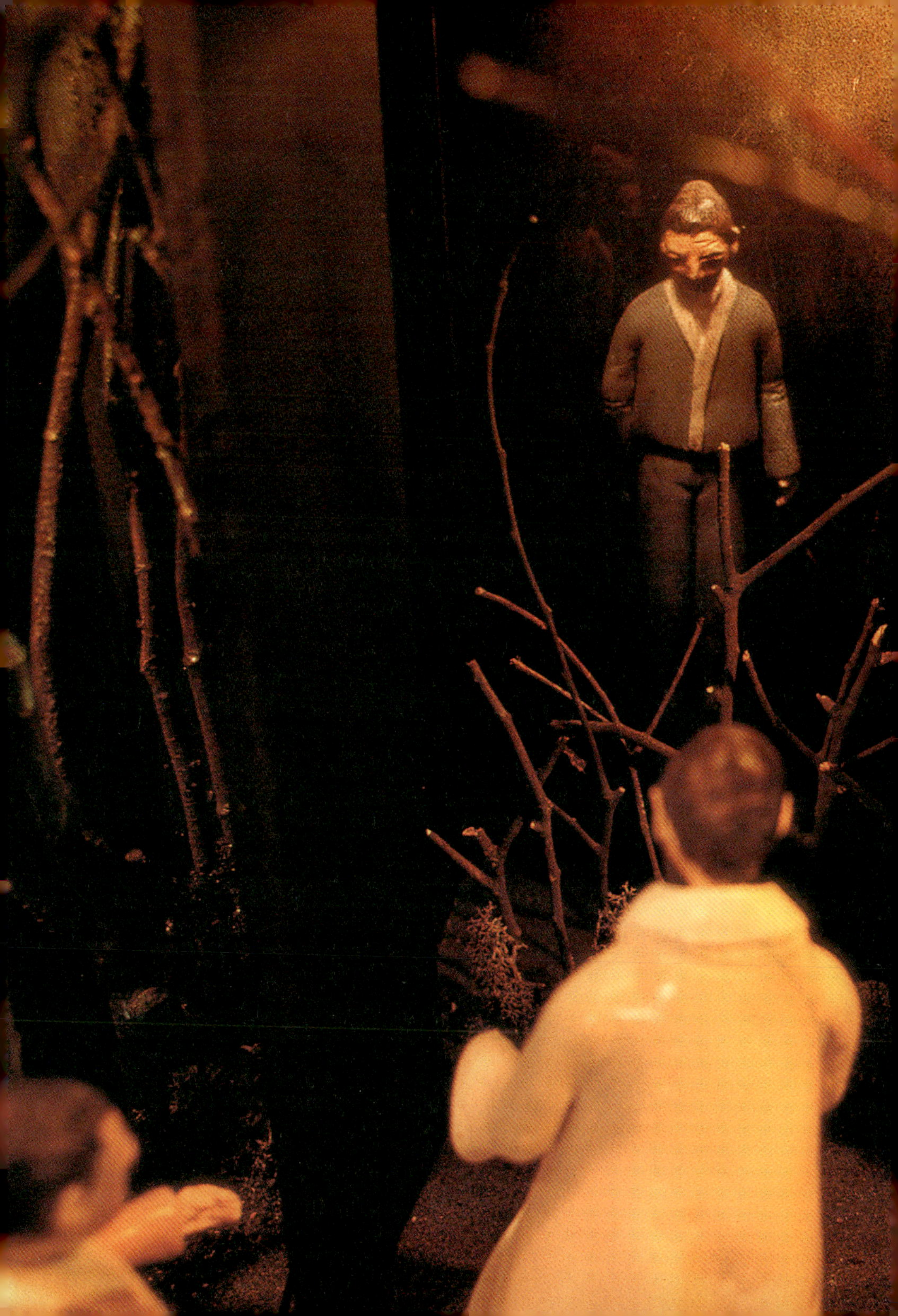

丘の上に着いたとき、
一行はふたたび林間の草地を眺めた。
すると一匹の虎が林間から躍り出るのを見た。
虎はすでに白く光を失った月を仰いで、
二声三声咆哮したかと思うと、またもとの草むらに踊り入って、
ふたたびその姿を見なかった。

When the group reached the top of the hill,
they looked back towards the forest path
and saw the tiger spring out from between the trees.
The tiger looked up at the already fading moon, and howled a few times.
Then he jumped back in the thicket, and was never seen again.

café inside
Sangetsu-Ki

Here Comes Gloria Maria | 1996
グロリア・マリアが来たりて | original sound: Muttoni
(keyboard, trumpet, sampled voice & sound effects)

café inside
Here Comes Gloria Maria

迷路のように入り組んだ路地。
突き当たりには、あやしげな教会。
人々は月に一度だけ行われる特別なミサに参列し、
自らの魂の捨て場を求める。

At the end of a labyrinth of alleys
stands a suspicious-looking church.
People attend a special mass there,
celebrated only once a month,
looking for a place to discard their souls.

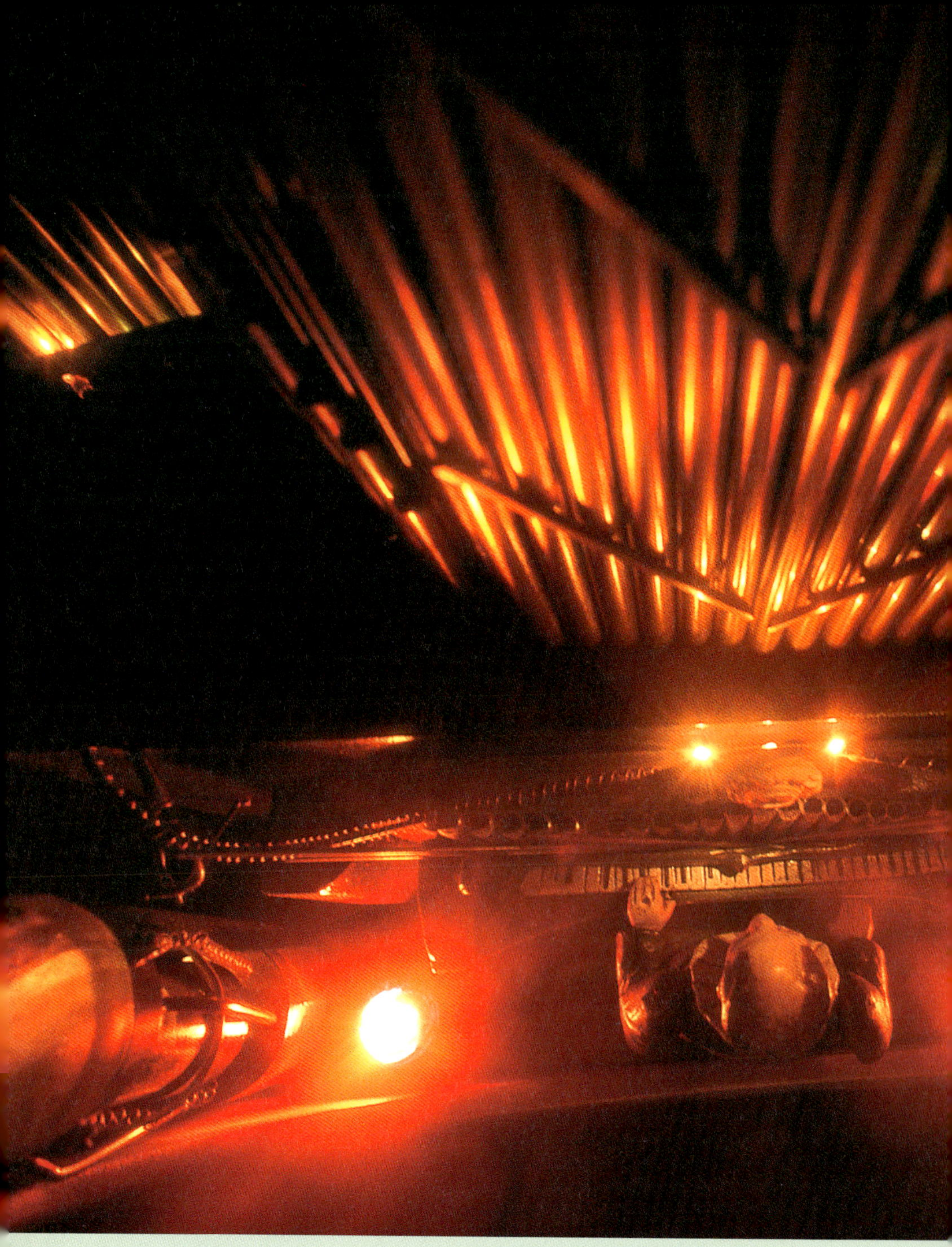

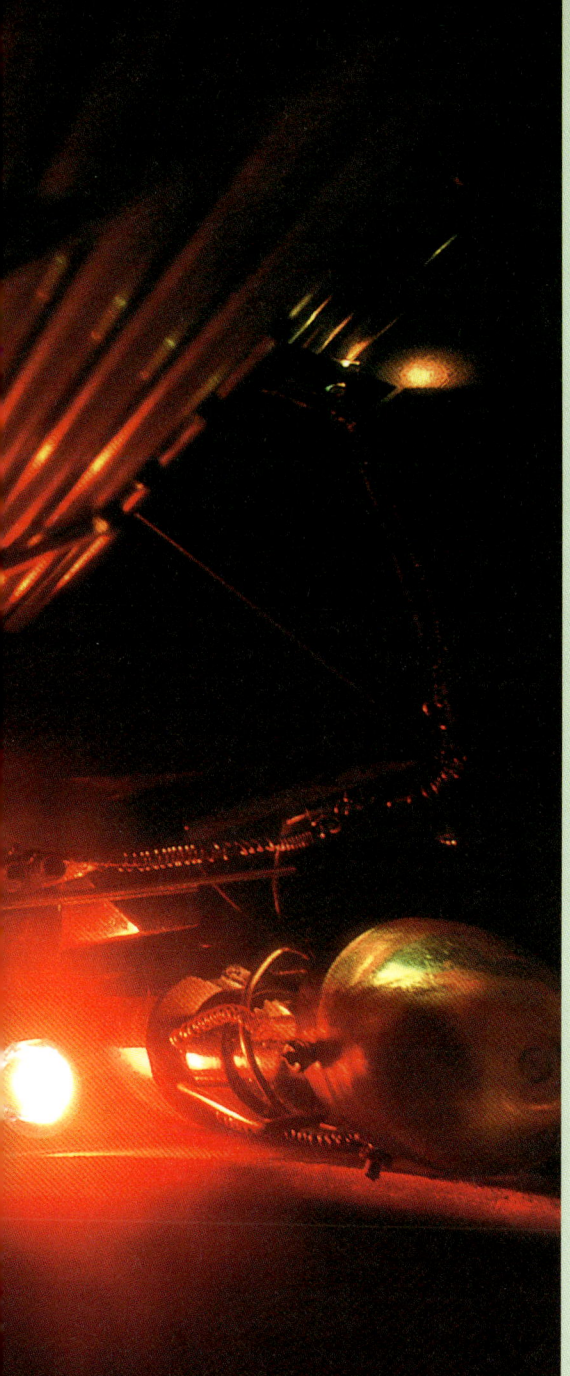

司祭はゆっくりと鍵盤に指を降ろす。
荘厳なパイプオルガンの調べが
あたりに沈黙をうながす。

The priest gently lays his fingers on the keyboard.
The notes of the majestic pipe organ
dispels the surrounding silence.

café inside
Here Comes Gloria Maria

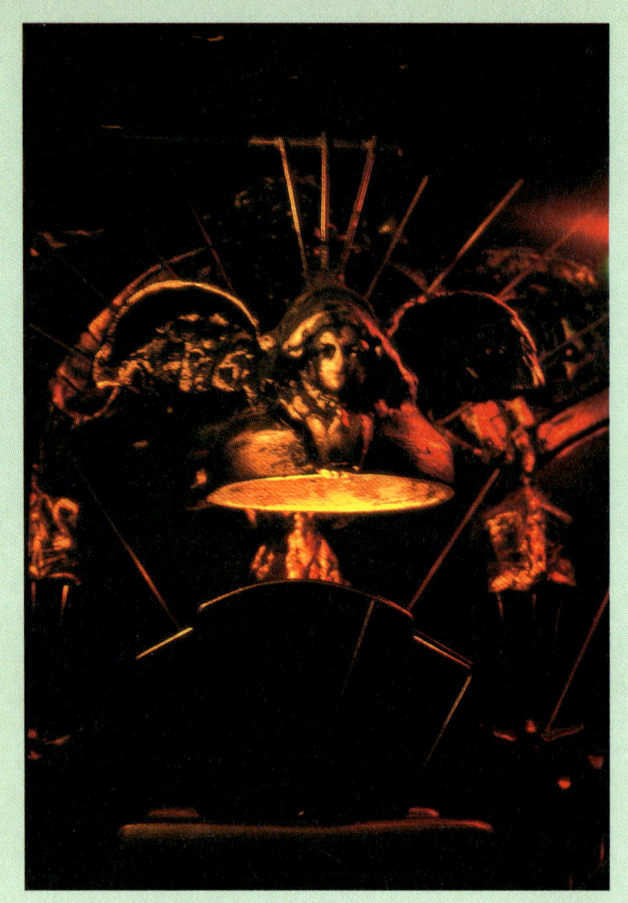

やがて賛美歌が歌われ、
天井から吊された鐘が鳴り響く中、
いよいよミサの幕が切って落とされる。

A hymn of praise is sung,
and as the bells in the ceiling chime,
the curtain rises for the mass.

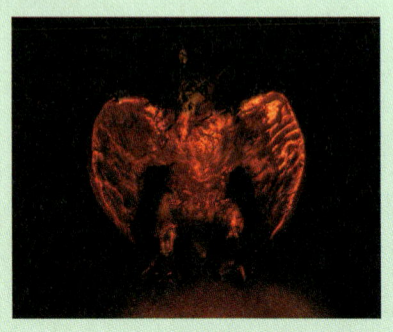

080
café inside
Here Comes Gloria Maria

パイプオルガンがゆっくりと割れ、
中から一人の乙女が姿をあらわす。

The organ pipes slowly part,
revealing a maiden.

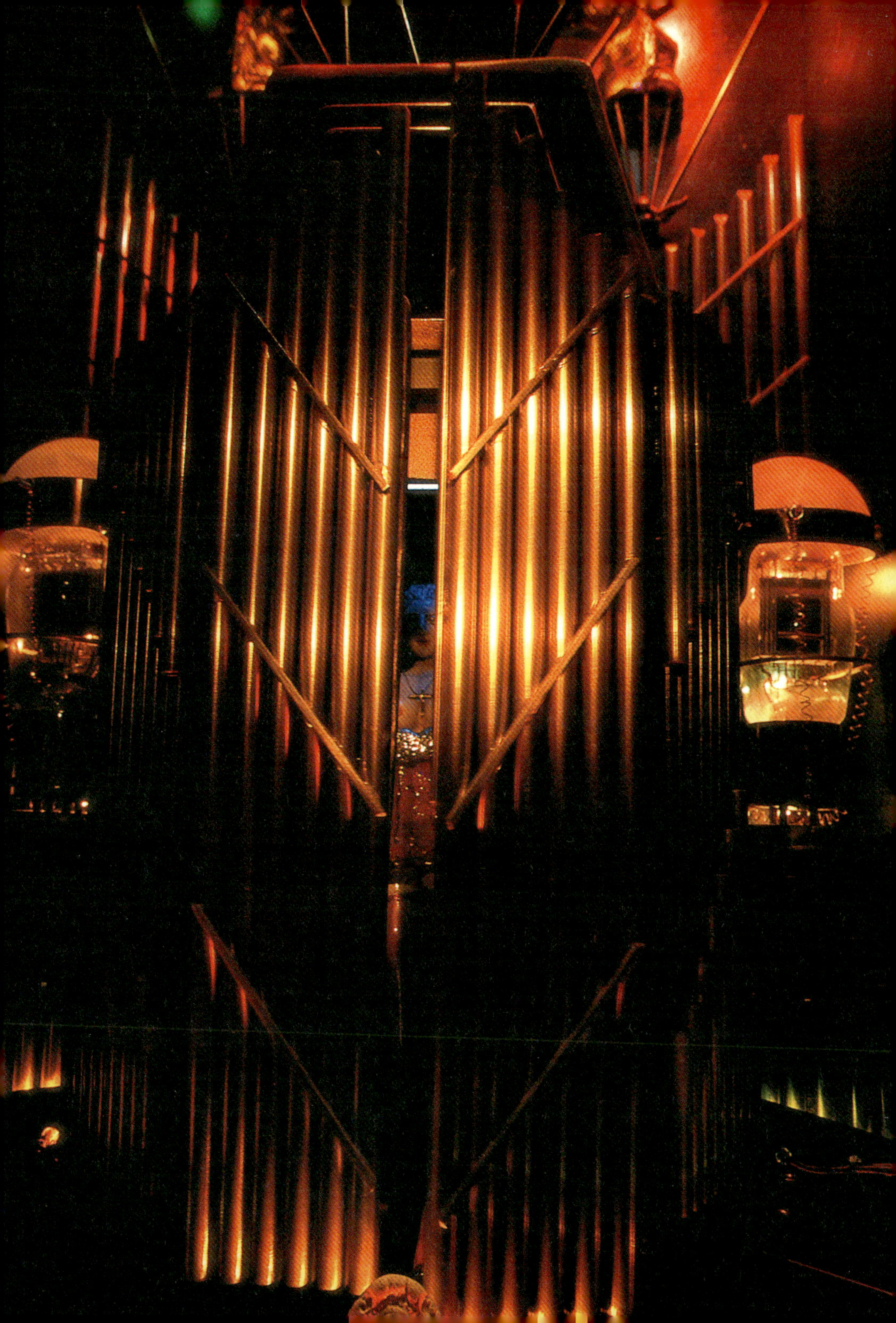

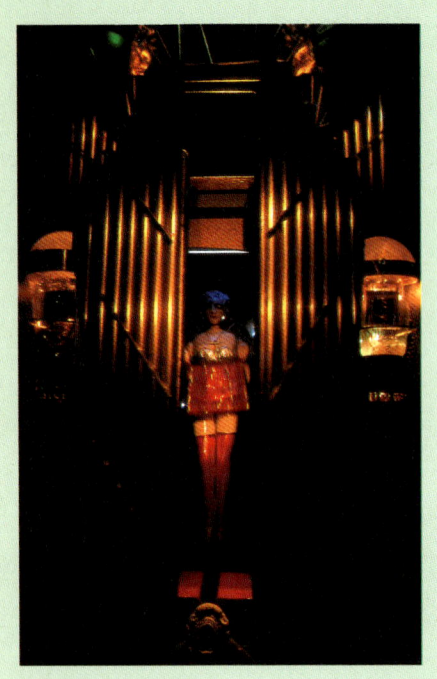

乙女は胸元にベールをかざし、
ゆっくりと信者の方へ歩み寄る。
そして、彼等の前に艶かしい肢体をさらけ出す。

The girl holds a veil in front of her chest.
Slowly she approaches the believers,
and exposes her alluring body.

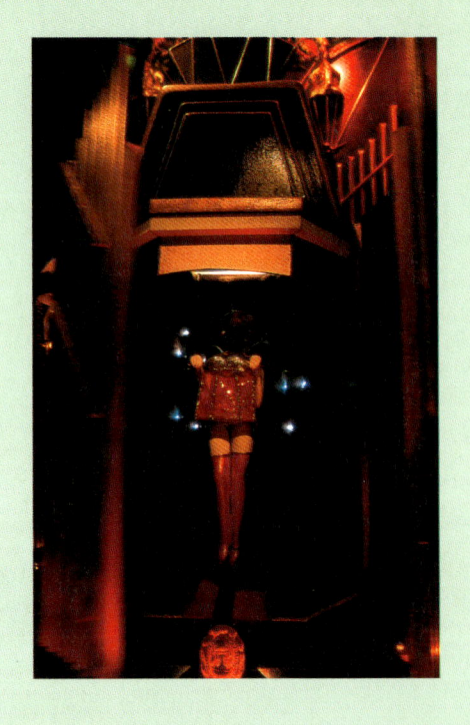

082
café inside
Here Comes Gloria Maria

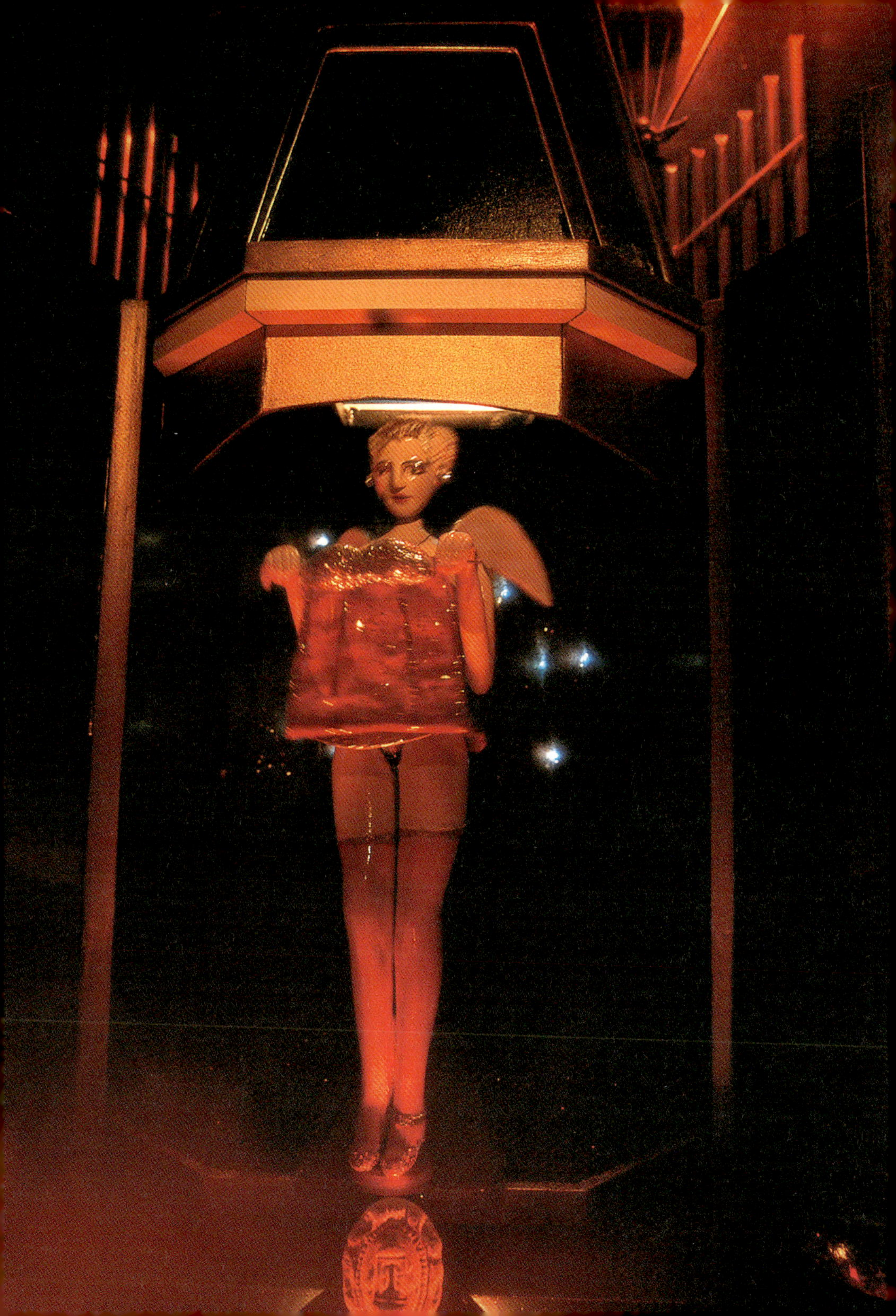

やがてミサ曲が絶頂を迎えると、
すべての音が止み、
突如訪れた束の間の沈黙の中で、
乙女はゆっくりとベールを降ろすのだ。

As the mass reaches its peak,
all sounds stop.
In the sudden quiet
she slowly lowers the veil.

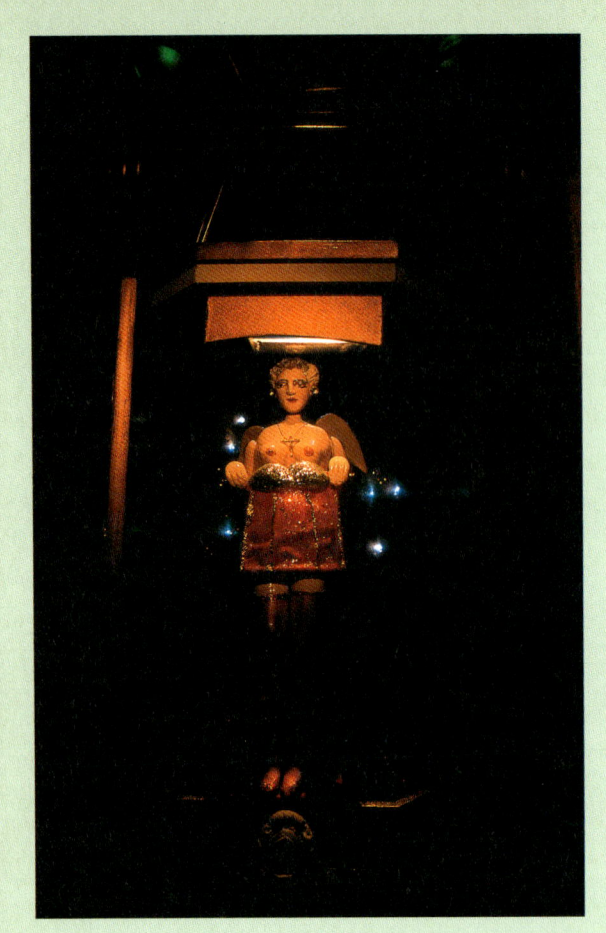

café inside
Here Comes Gloria Maria

しかし、それらの一切、
この教会の存在そのものは、路地裏に堆積した魂たちが
生み出した幻影だったのかもしれない。

But perhaps all of this,
even the very existence of the church itself,
is just a dream dreamt by the discarded souls
piling up in the backstreets.

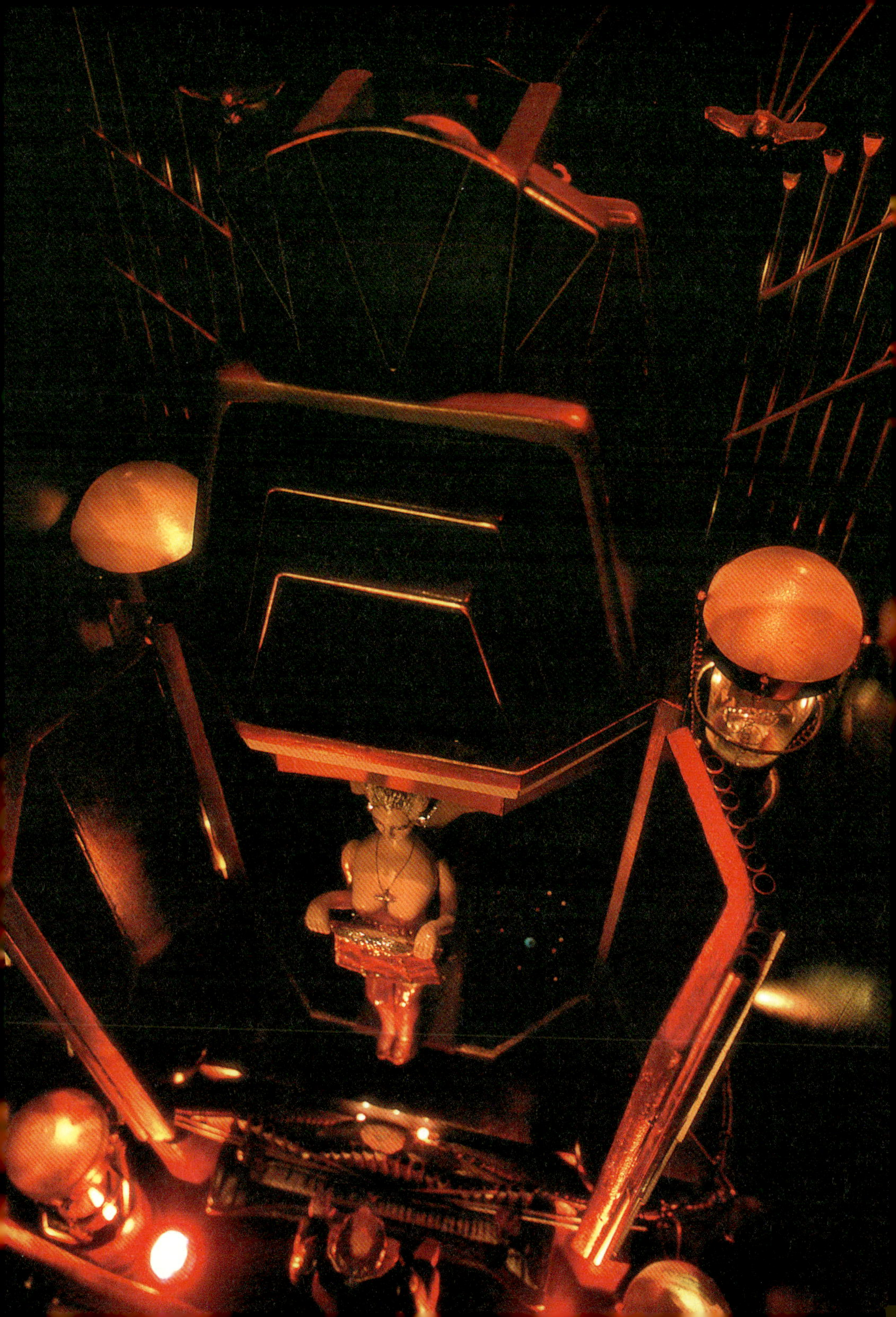

Last Supper
ドラキュラの晩餐

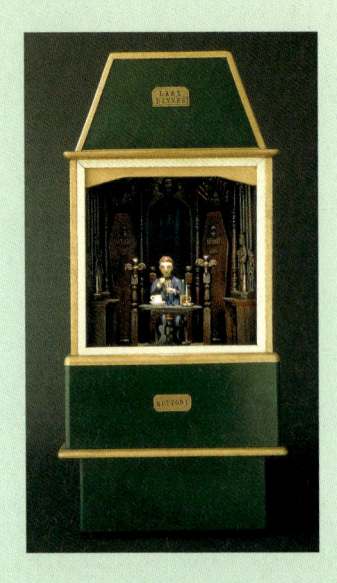

1998
original sound: Muttoni
(keyboard, sampling & sound effects)
owned by: Yamaguchi Jun

まもなく背後で何かが軋む音が。
男が後ろを振り返ると……。

Behind him he hears a creaking noise,
and as he turns around...

086
café inside
Last Supper

怪しげな屋敷に招かれた男は、
用意された晩餐を終え、主人の到来を待っていた。
不気味な気配が漂う中、何処からともなく鼓動が響いてくる。

A man has been invited to a queer residence.
While waiting for his host to arrive,
he finishes the meal that has been prepared for him.
With an eerie mood drifting through the room,
somewhere a beating drum is heard.

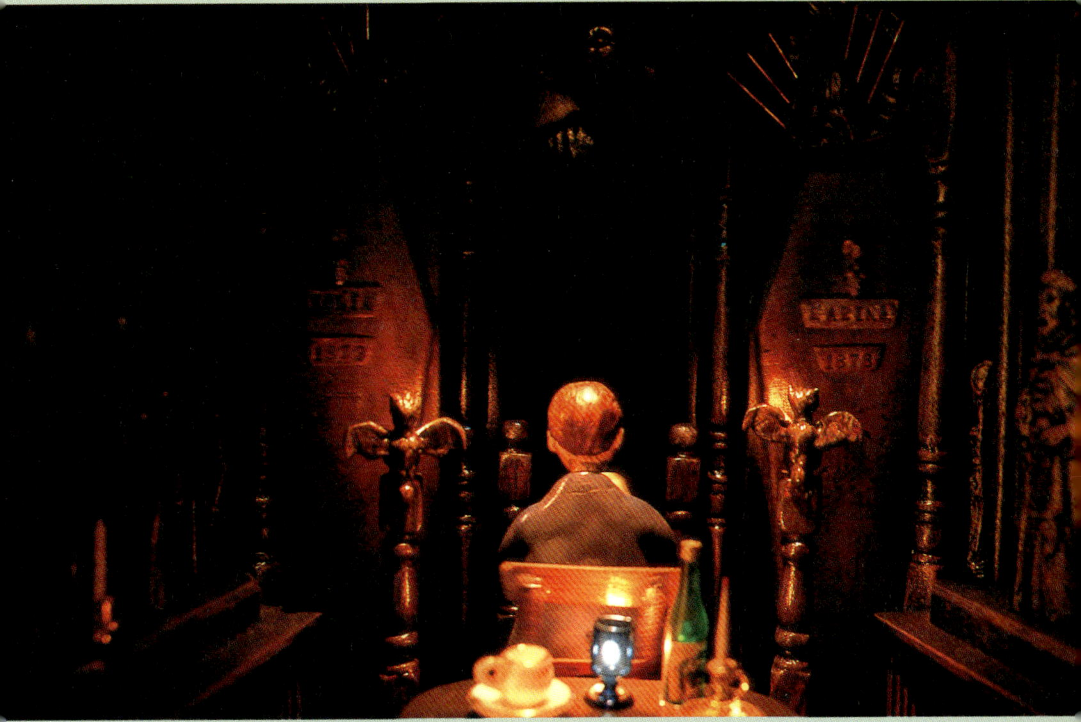

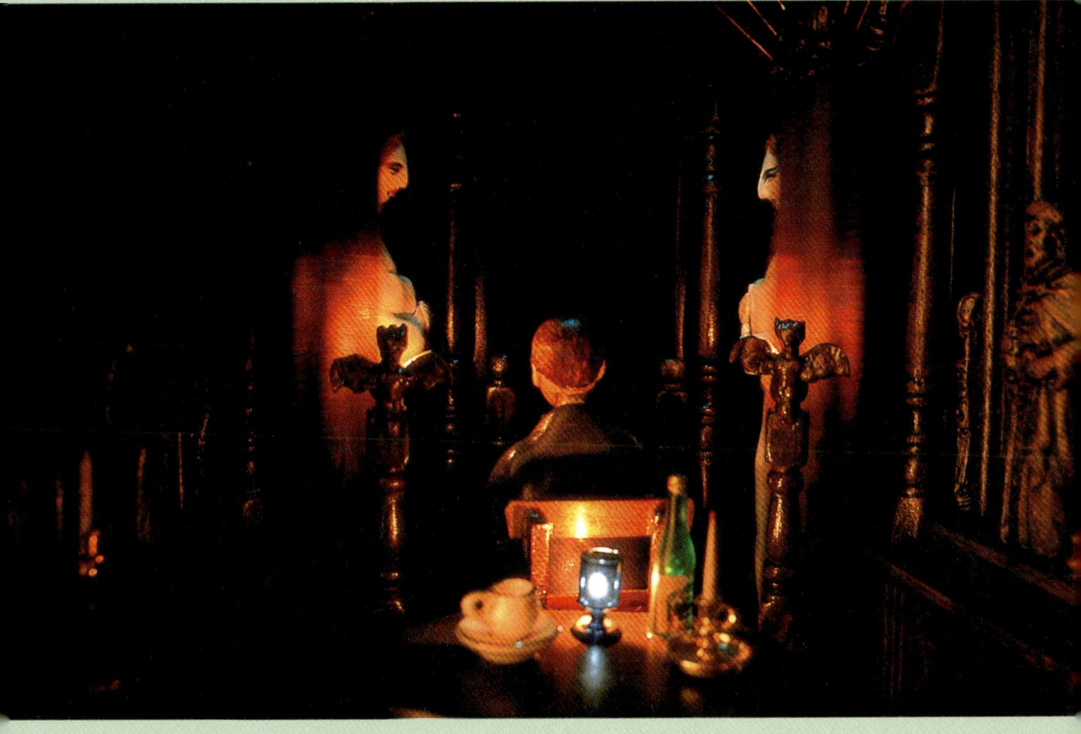

088
café inside
Last Supper

棺の裏から二人の僕が姿をあらわし、
その奥に黒いシルエットが浮かび上がった。

Two servants appear from their caskets,
and behind them a black silhouette starts to materialize.

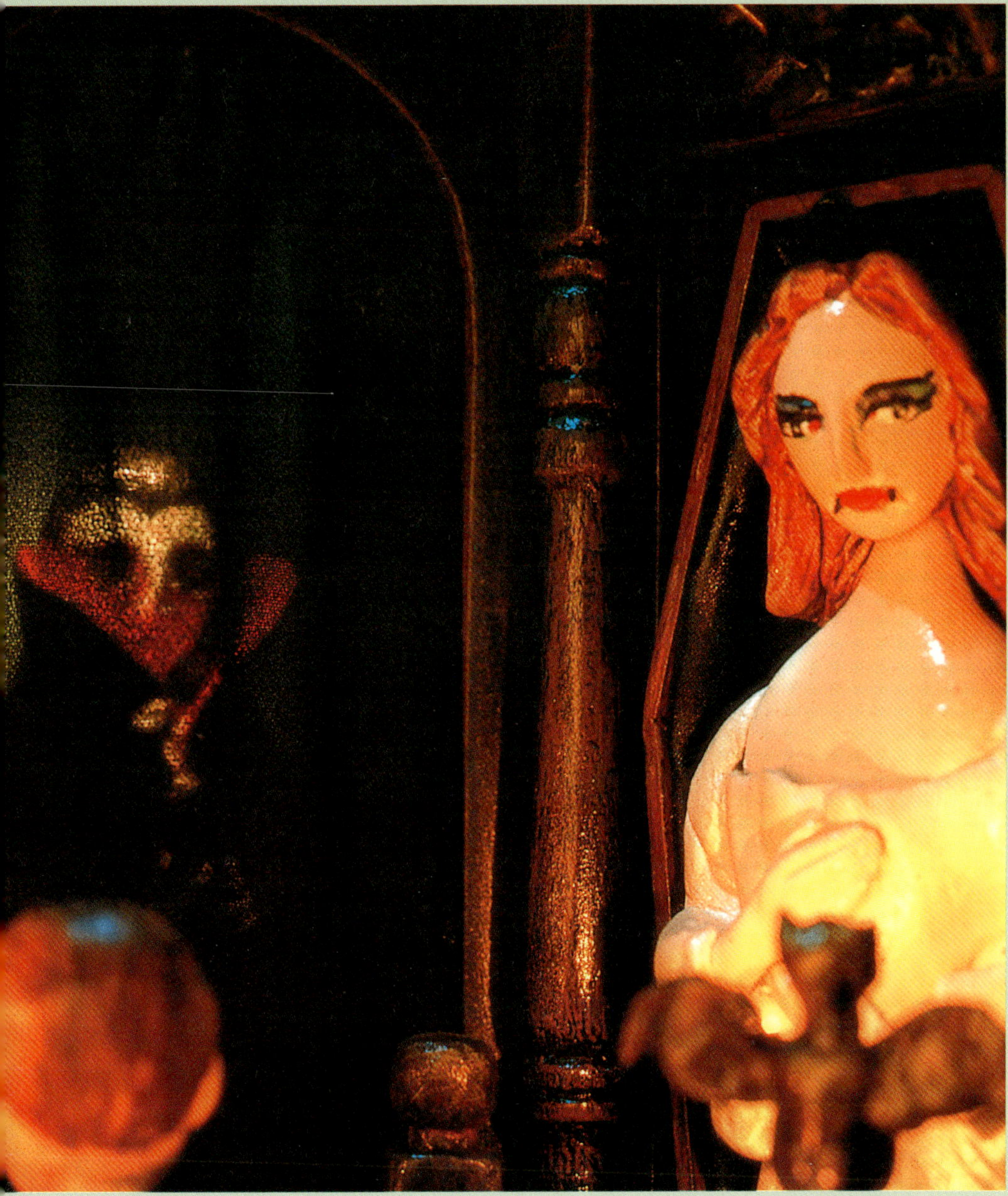

雷の光によって浮かび上がったその主人が、
男に向かって告げる。
「ラスト・ディナー。
最後の餌食は、お前自身……」

With a flash the host arrives and tells the man:
"The last supper. Tonight's final dish is *you*..."

Return Home
透明人間の帰還

1998
sound: Patti Page "It's A Sin To Tell A Lie"
 with Muttoni's footsteps
owned by: Aramata Hiroshi

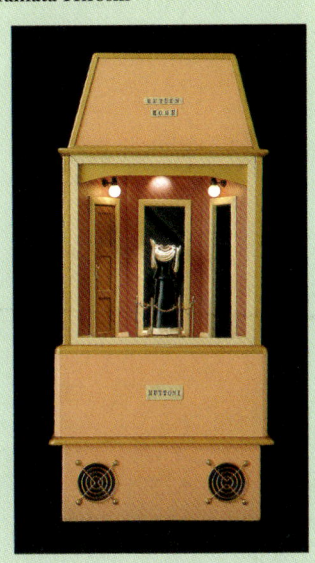

男は何年かぶりに家へ帰ってきた。
しかし彼の姿はなく、靴音だけが響く。

A man returns home after many years.
However, you cannot see him,
only hear his shoes.

091
café inside
Return Home

見慣れた室内。
妻の姿はなく、
歌手だった彼女の最後の衣装が飾られているだけ。
靴音は衣装の前で止まった。
突然、スポットライトがともり、
ドレスだけがゆっくりと踊りはじめる。

A familiar room.
But his wife, who used to be a singer, is not there.
Only the dress she wore for her last show is on display.
The footsteps stop in front of the dress.
Suddenly, a spotlight turns on
and the dress slowly starts to dance all by itself.

café inside
Return Home

この真夜中の異変に気づいたのは、
ただひとりのもの。

Only one is watching
these strange goings-on in the night.

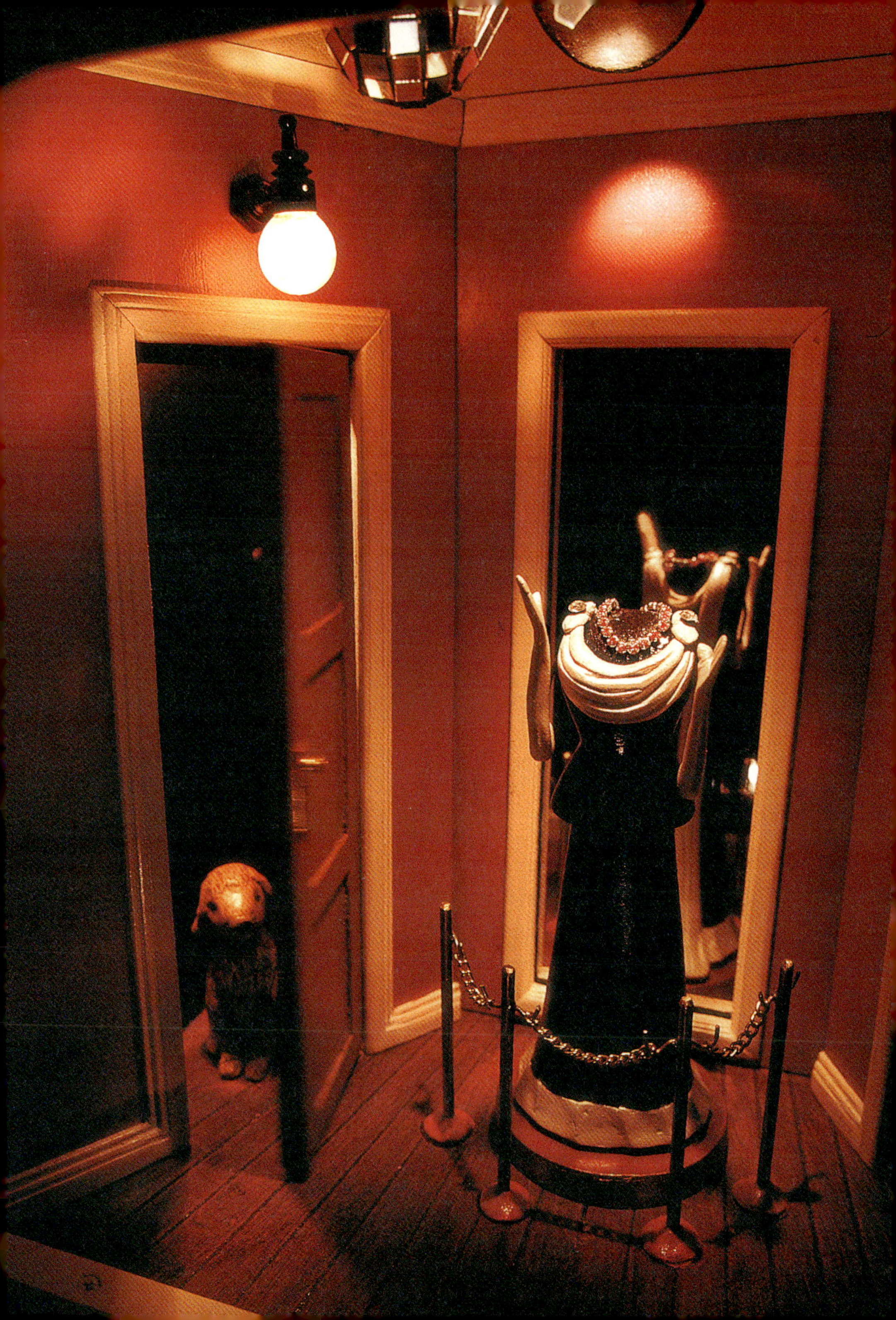

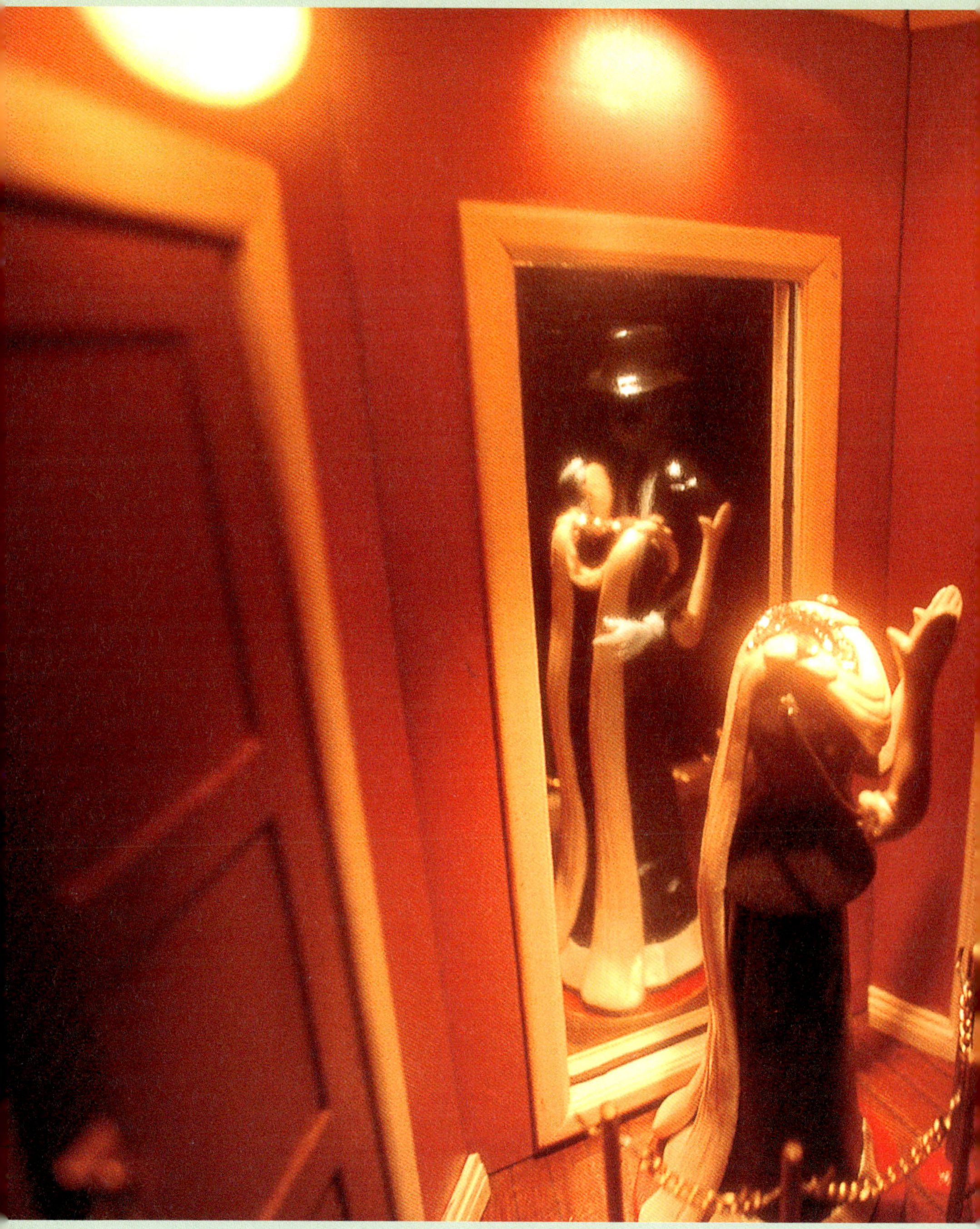

老犬の出迎えを受け、
男は一瞬、鏡の中に姿をあらわす。
鏡の中だけの抱擁、最後のチークダンス。

Welcomed by his old dog,
the man briefly appears in the mirror.
An embrace for the mirror,
and a final cheek-to-cheek dance.

café inside
Return Home

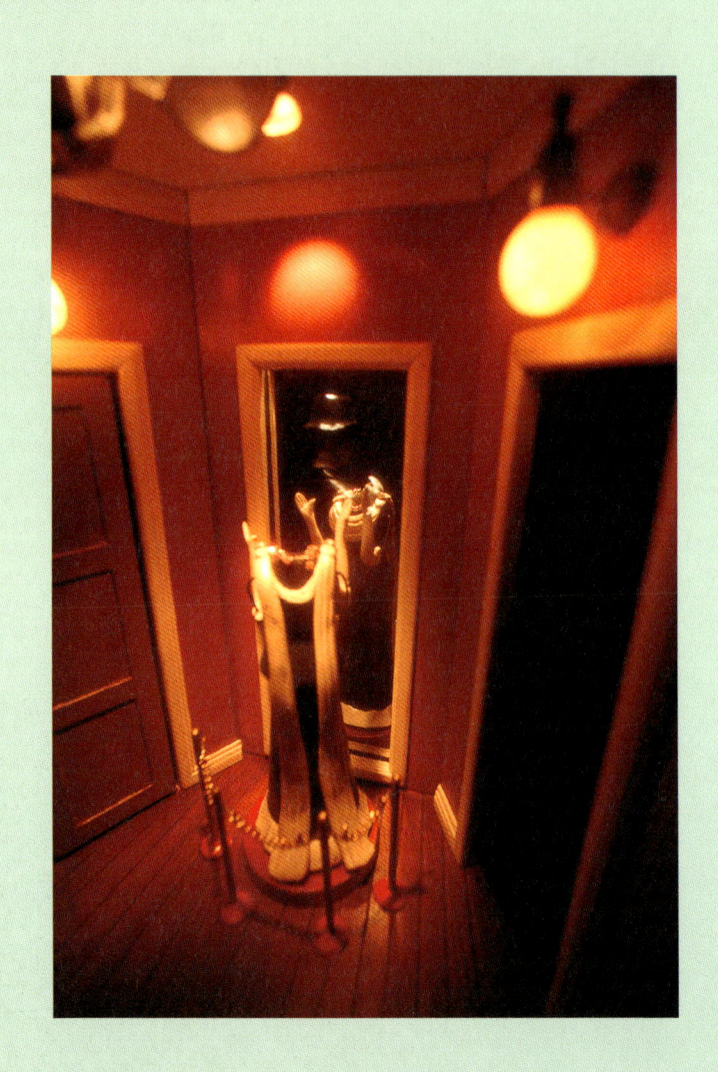

096
café inside
Return Home

静寂が戻った室内に、靴音が響く。
帰りぎわに男は、妻の面影に別れを告げた。

The room has returned to stillness, and only the footsteps are heard.
As he leaves, the man bids farewell to the image of his wife.

café inside
Return Home

Bunny's Memory
バニーズ・メモリー

1996
sound: Modern Playboys "Harlem Nocturne"

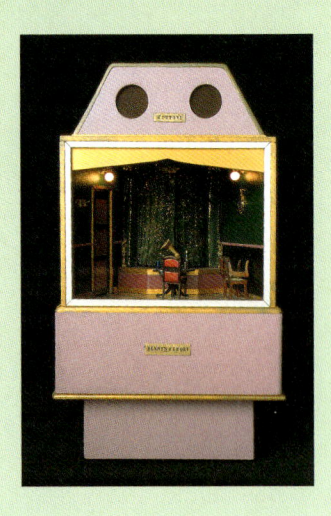

場末のミュージックホールの演目は、
想い出で組み立てた一幕劇。
月のない夜、失われた記憶の謎が解きあかされる。

On the program in a music hall on the outskirts of town
is a nostalgic one-act play.
On this moonless night, riddles of lost memories will be solved.

098
café inside
Bunny's Memory

夜想曲の旋律とともにゆっくりカーテンが開き、
あやしげなミュージシャンがあらわれる。

To the tune of a nocturne, the curtain slowly opens,
and a mysterious musician appears.

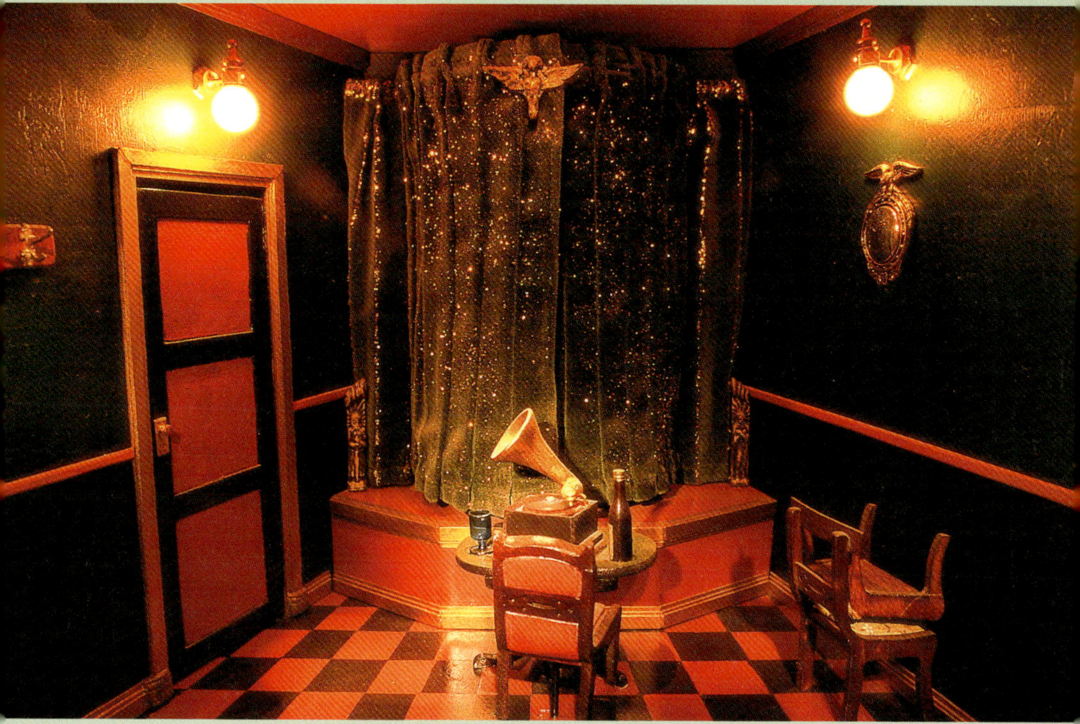

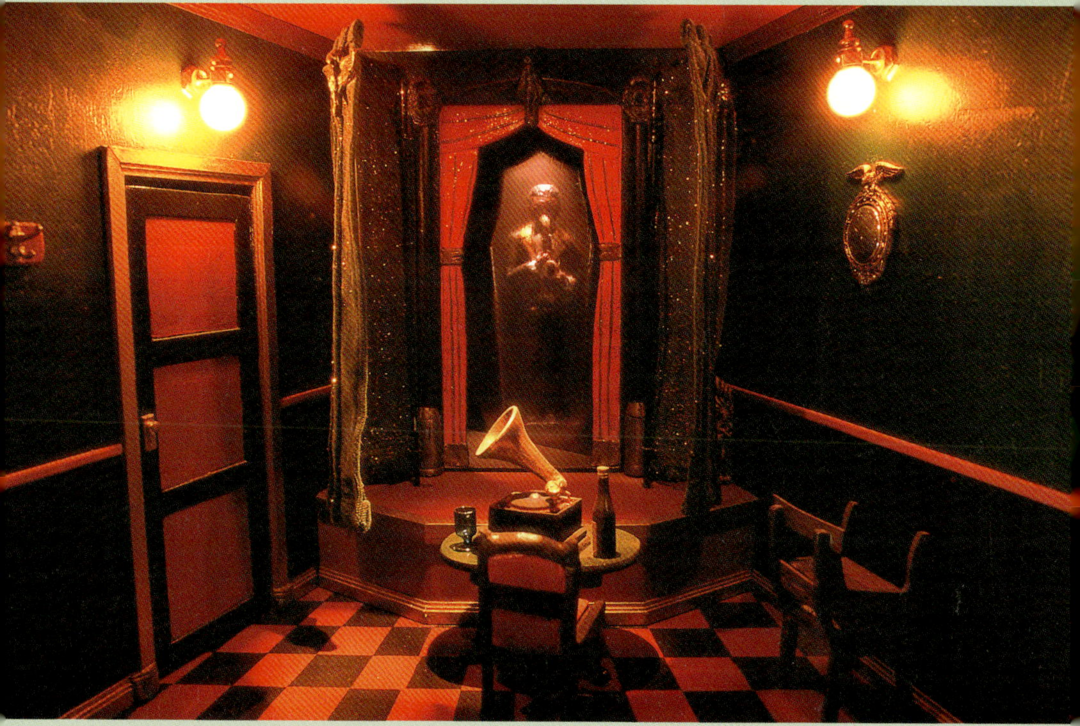

舞台は回転し、今宵の主役のバニーガールが登場。
スポットライトが回る中、彼女は踊りはじめる。

100
café inside
Bunny's Memory

The stage turns, and tonight's star appears — the bunny girl.
In the rotating spotlight, she starts to dance.

回る舞台。
めぐるスポットライト。
そして擦り切れたSP盤の回転。
三つの輪舞が一つに重なり合ったとき、
バニーガールの姿は揺らぎはじめる。

A turning stage.
Rotating spotlights.
And then the revolving worn-out 78 record.
As these three cycles coincide
the bunny girl begins to fade.

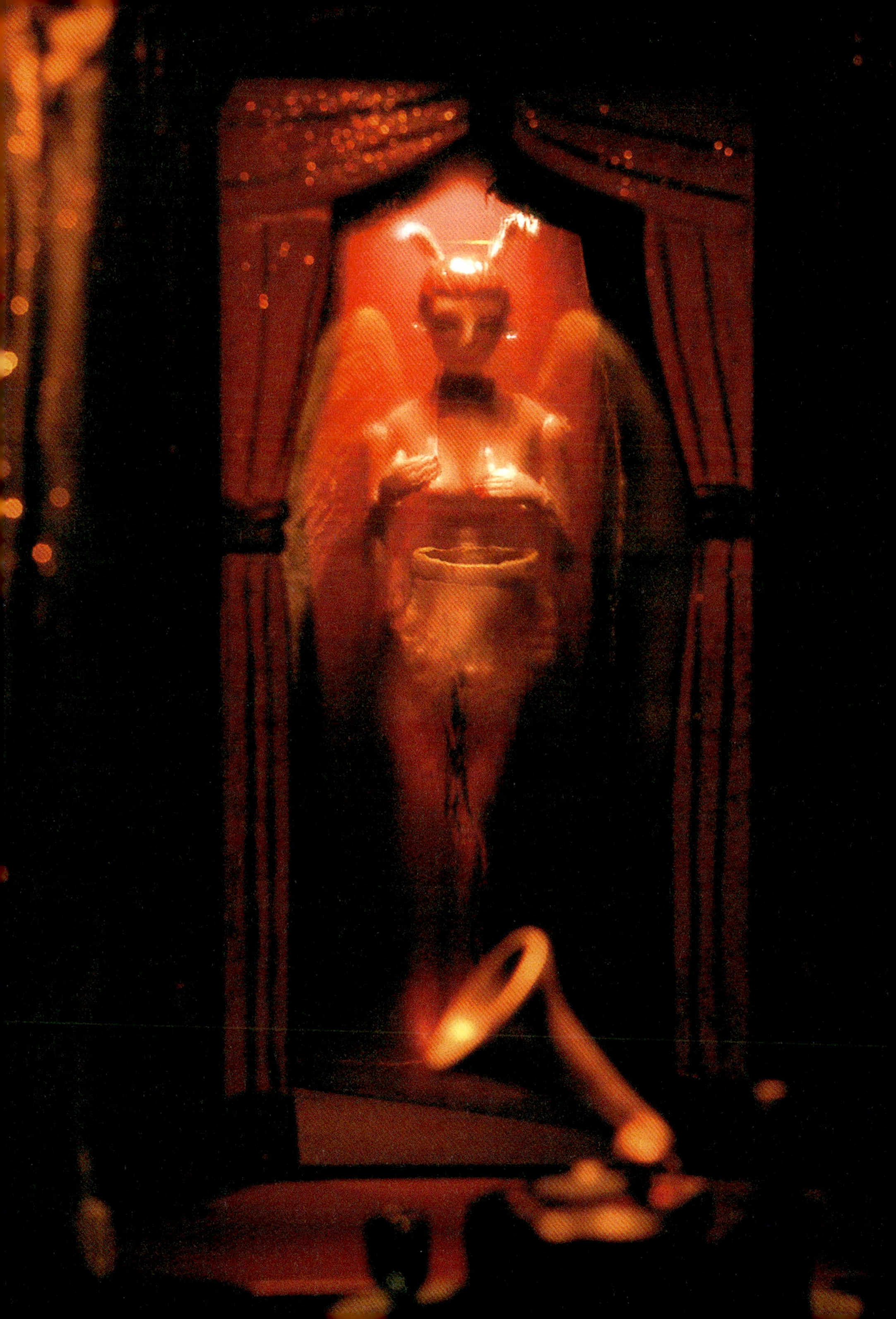

彼女は一瞬、翼を得る。
翼とエプロンをステージに残して、とうとう自由の身に……。
背中に刻印を刻まれた彼女が、扰の外に立つ。

For a moment she has wings.
Leaving her apron and the wings behind on the stage,
she is free at last...
With marks carved into her back, she stands outside the door.

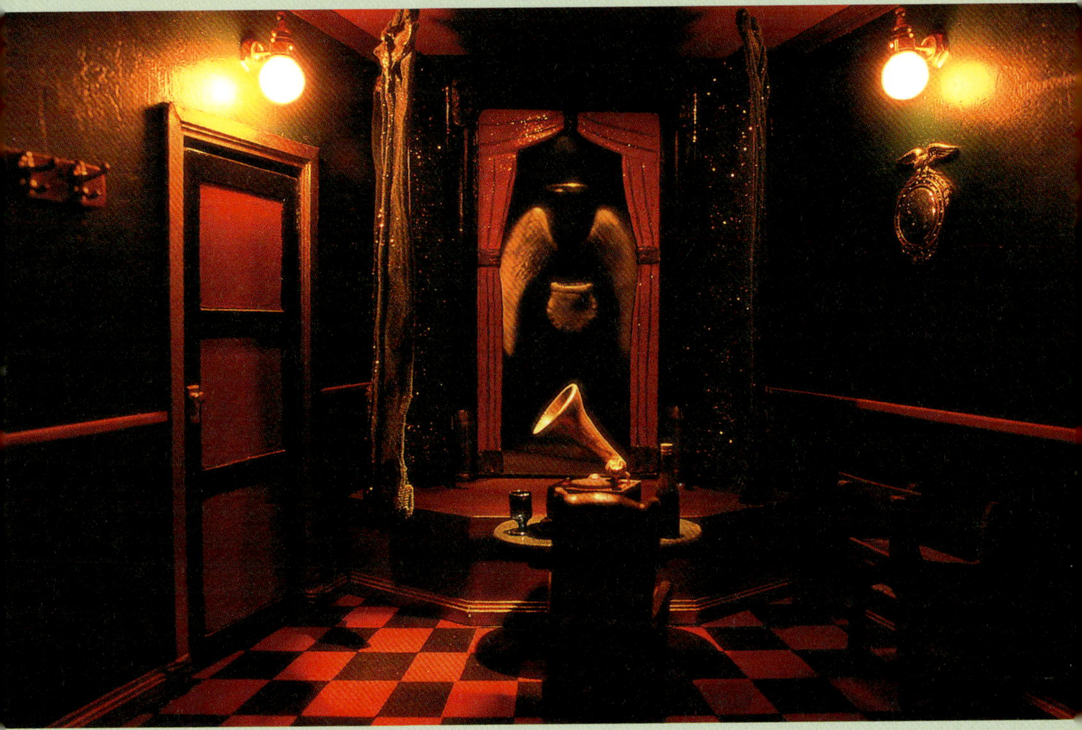

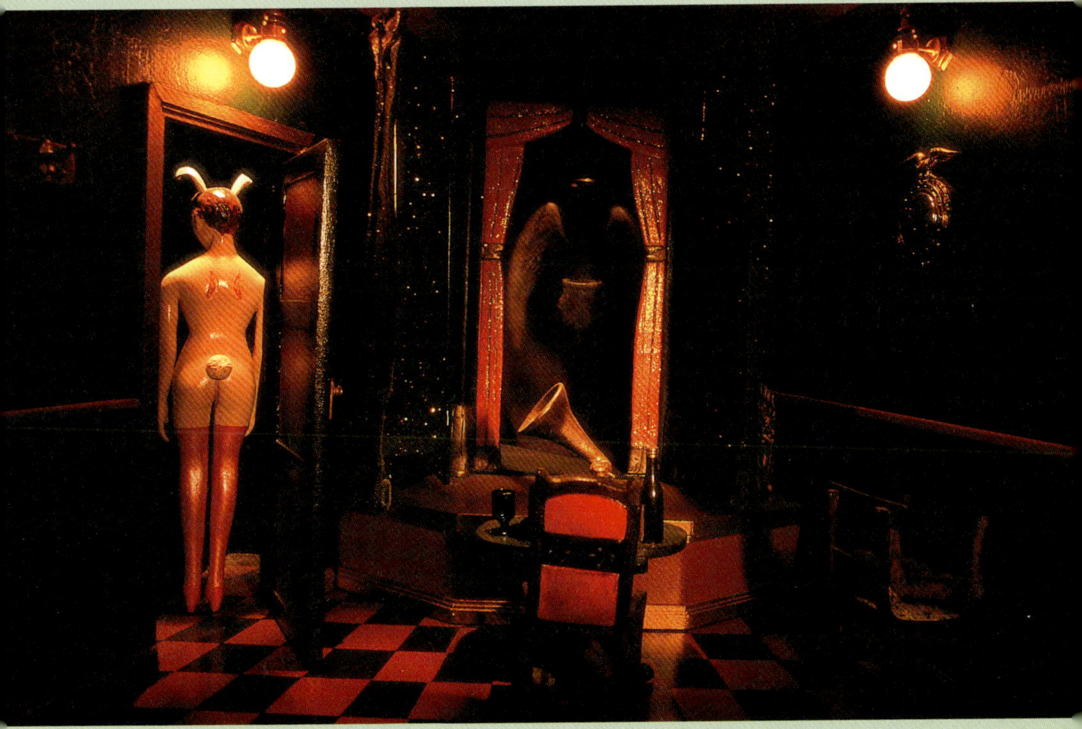

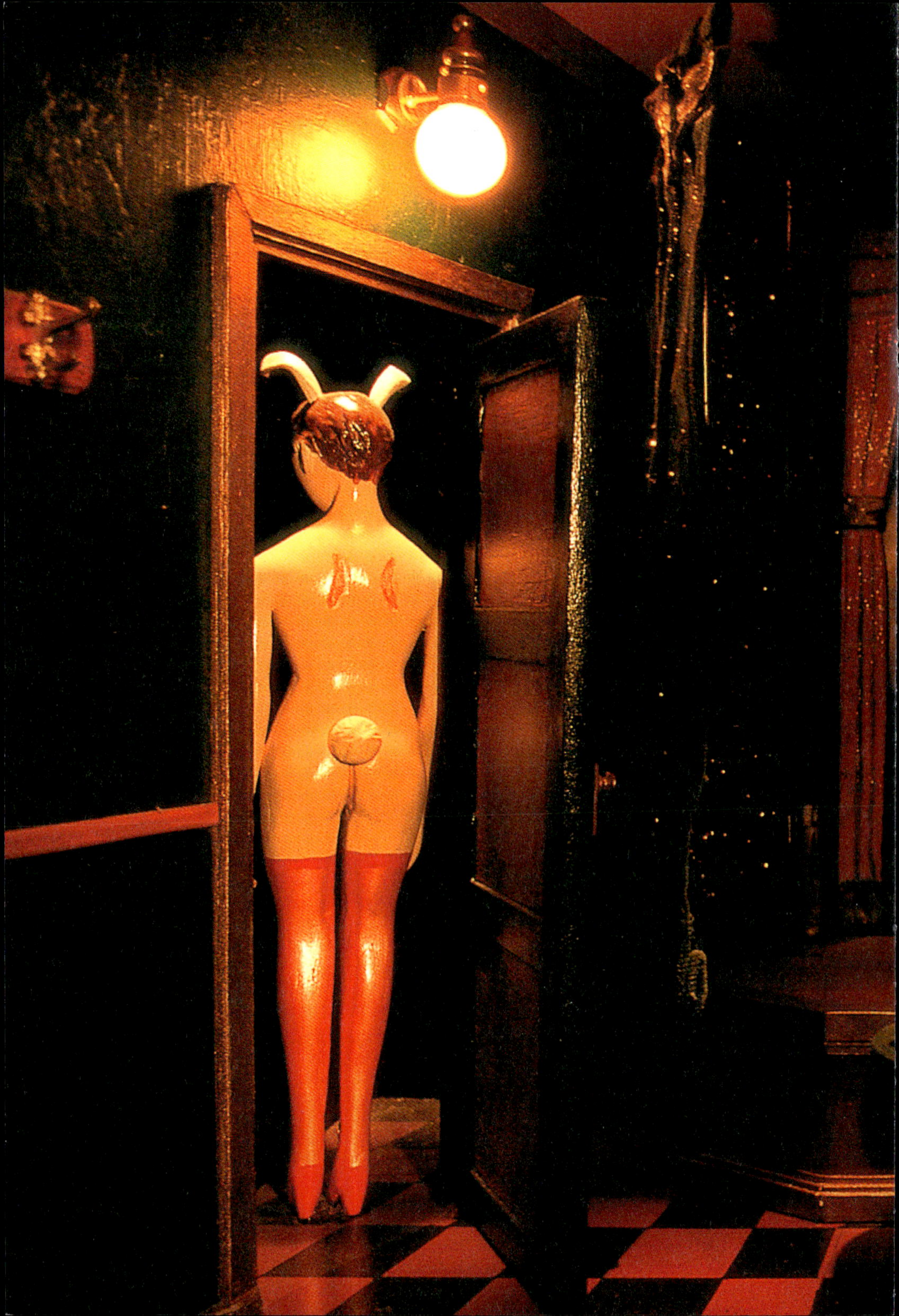

しかし、ドラマは終わらない。
本当の主人公。
それはショーの一部始終を見ていた椅子の上の彼女。

But the drama is not over yet.
The real protagonist is her bunny self on the chair,
who has been watching this part from beginning to end.

すべてはSP盤に刻まれた想い出、
永遠にこの舞台で繰り返される運命なのだ。

All these are memories engraved onto the 78 record,
destined to endlessly repeat themselves on this stage.

café inside
Bunny's Memory

"Good night..."

CAST

Arnold and Margarita
a boy and a girl
Luis Leloir
Marina Scholl
Emilia Maetzel
Helen Morgan
Elize Carlos
Eugena
Maria
Gabriel Rossetti and Conti
Otto Behaghel
Pepi
Constantino
Behaim
Michurin
Teromea
Makarios
Jorge Luis Borgesso
a man
Lichou and Ensan
Fernand Gallego and Santa Catarina
Marina and Gloria
Robert
Velora

afterword

私は時々考える。あのウサギになり代わって、バニーズ・メモリーを見ることができたら……。きっとミュージシャンはもっと不気味で、バニーガールはもっと神秘的に見えるだろう。舵を取るアンドロイドもいい。宇宙の中心から眺めた世界の美しさと、自分が中心にいることの孤独さを、はっきり知ることが出来るだろう。世界に光を投げかけるビィーナス。天使の翼に抱かれた歌姫。でも、あの皿の上の猫だけにはなりたくない。あんな所で一生グルグル回ってはいられない。

でも良く考えてみると、彼等の場所に立ったときに一番良く見えるのは、その世界をのぞき込んでいる私たちの顔ということにはならないだろうか？　だとするとステージの中をグルグル回っている猫の方が、その世界を360°堪能できる。だがもし、皿が横を向いたときにネジが切れたら……。目の前の壁をじーっと見つめたまま、気まぐれな主人がゼンマイを巻くのを待たなければならない。

やはり私は人形にはなりたくない。作っているだけで充分なのだ。

武藤政彦　1999.12

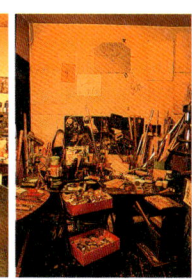

Sometimes I think, what if I could be that rabbit and watch the bunny girl's memories... I guess the musician would look even weirder and the bunny girl even more mysterious. The steering android wouldn't be bad either — to be able to see the beauty of the world from the center of the universe, and to feel the loneliness of being at the center. Or Venus, illuminating the world. Or the singer wrapped in angel wings. But I definitely wouldn't want to be the cat on the plate and spend all my life spinning around like that.

Come to think about it, wouldn't the most striking objects from the dolls' point of view be our faces peeping into their world? In that case, the cat on his revolving stage would be able to see 360 degrees around him. But what if the spring wound down just when the plate is tilted sideways. Then he would have to keep staring at the wall in front of him until his capricious master would deign to wind up the spring again.

No, I wouldn't want to be a doll after all. I'm happy just making them.

MUTTONI 1999.12

profile

武藤政彦
Muto Masahiko (Muttoni)

1956年生まれ。少年時代、日々夕日の町中をさまよう。そこで見たり感じとったりした物を油粘土でジオラマ化していた。十代半ばから油彩画を描きはじめ、美術学校を経て平面絵画に専念する。のちに人形制作を手掛け、15年前それまでの要素をまとめた「自動カラクリお話し玉手箱」なる物の制作に没頭、現在に至る。
Born in 1956. Spent his youth wandering about town day and night, and making clay dioramas of what he saw and felt. Took up oil painting in his late teens, and after graduating from art school concentrated on painting. Later began making dolls, and about 15 years ago developed his own style of "Mechanical Fairy Boxes."

★主な展覧会
1987、88　　青木画廊
1995　　　　有楽町マリオン、阪急ギャラリー
1995、96　　東京ガスTSSホール
1995-2000　渋谷パルコ、ロゴスギャラリー
1997　　　　ラフォーレミュージアム原宿
1997-98　　西日本各地を巡回
　　　　　　　　　　　　その他

★公共施設作品所蔵リスト

世田谷文学館
東京都世田谷区南烏山1-10-10　phone: 03-5374-9111

鳥取わらべ館
鳥取市西町3-202　phone: 0857-22-7070

牧野富太郎記念館
高知市五台山3579-2　phone: 0888-82-2601

ムットーニ・カフェ

発行日	2000年2月10日
著者	武藤政彦
撮影	佐々木 光
撮影協力	今井紀彰＋升平香織
翻訳	ヤーン・フォルネル
編集	米澤 敬
アート・ディレクション	松田行正
エディトリアル・デザイン	澤地真由美
制作協力	荒俣 宏＋山口 旬＋山口由子＋齋藤直子＋世田谷文学館
印刷・製本	文唱堂印刷株式会社
発行者	中上千里夫
発行	工作舎 editorial corporation for human becoming
	〒150-0046 東京都渋谷区松濤2-21-3 phone:03-3465-5251 fax: 03-3465-5254
	URL http://www.kousakusha.co.jp e-mail: saturn@kousakusha.co.jp
	ISBN4-87502-323-5

MUTTONI Café by Muto Masahiko

photography	Sasaki Hikaru
photography cooperation	Imai Noriaki＋Masuhira Kaori
translation	Jan Fornell
editing	Yonezawa Kei
art direction	Matzda Yukimasa
editorial design	Sawachi Mayumi
special thanks	Aramata Hiroshi＋Yamaguchi Jun＋Yamaguchi Yuko＋Saito Naoko＋
	Setagaya Literary Museum
printing & bookbinding	Bunshodo Printing
publisher	Nakagami Chisao

Japanese edition©2000 by Kousakusha, Shoto 2-21-3, Shibuya-ku, Tokyo, Japan 150-0046